Sheltered by the King

Sheltered
by the
King

by
Marta Gabre-Tsadick
with
Sandra Picklesimer Aldrich

√Chosen Books, Lincoln, Virginia 22078
of The Zondervan Corporation, Grand Rapids, Michigan 49506

iii

Library of Congress Cataloging in Publication Data

Gabre-Tsadick, Marta.
  Sheltered by the king.

  1. Gabre-Tsadick, Marta. 2. Ethiopia—History—Revolu-
tion, 1974—Personal narratives. 3. Legislators—Ethiopia—Bi-
ography. 4. Refugees—Political—Ethiopia—Biography. 5.
Refugees—Political—United States—Biography. I. Aldrich,
Sandra Picklesimer. II. Title.
DT387.954.G3A37 1982 963'.06 82-14675
ISBN 0-310-60400-1

Printed in the United States of America.

Chosen Books is a division of The Zondervan Corporation,
Grand Rapids, Michigan 49506. Editorial offices for Chosen
Books are in Lincoln, Virginia 22078.

Foreword

"I will never leave you nor forsake you," promised the Lord God to Joshua. In Sheltered by the King, Marta Gabre-Tsadick records the extraordinary pilgrimage of one family which is indisputable confirmation of God's faithfulness—God's unceasing, unfaltering, relentless care for His own. As one reads, he is reminded over and over again of Paul's declaration of God's unconditional, safe, triumphant love in his letter to the believers in Rome.

Richard C. Halverson
Chaplain
United States Senate

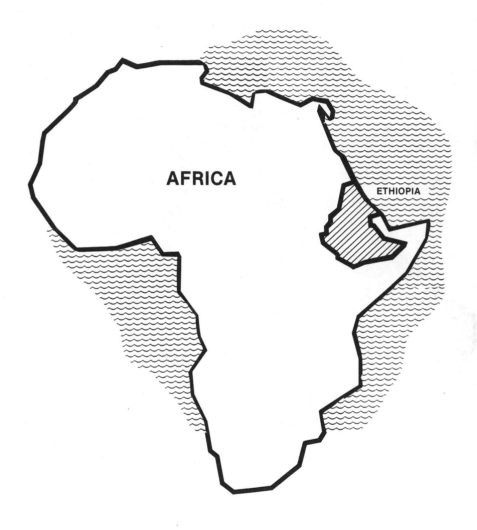

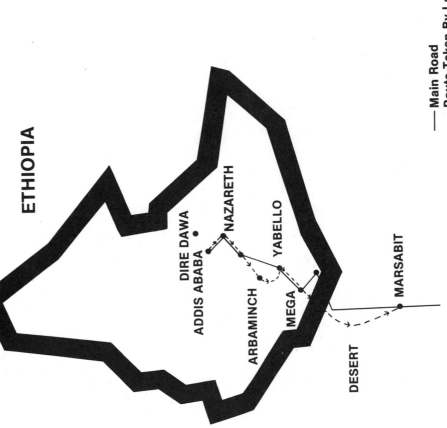

ETHIOPIA

DIRE DAWA

ADDIS ABABA

NAZARETH

YABELLO

ARBAMINCH

MEGA

MARSABIT

DESERT

—— Main Road
---- Route Taken By Land Rover

In a few cases in this manuscript, names and identifying details have been changed to protect families who might otherwise be hurt.

Chapter One

In my groggy passage from dreams to wakefulness, I couldn't remember why I was dreading the day. Then as awareness arrived I wanted to squeeze my eyes shut again. At nine o'clock I would be in His Majesty's office. Would he listen to my fears about our beloved Ethiopia?

I tossed the covers aside and groped for my slippers, my eyes on the rain-streaked window beside the bed. The rains in my country start in July and in this year of 1974 they were unwelcome since they blocked efforts to get grain out of the city and into the famine-stricken provinces north of the capital, Addis Ababa. If only we could have gotten the grain into the famine area before the rains sealed off the ancient roads . . . . If only we had more planes . . . . If only we had more time . . . .

I began to dress while practicing what I would say to His Majesty. But would I convince the Father of Africa that our country was heading toward disaster? Even though he had honored me by appointing me the first woman to serve in the Ethiopian Senate, I doubted he would take my warning seriously. What if he laughed at my distrust of the Committee, which was demanding more and more power? How could I make him see we were dealing with a regime that was as deadly as the famine?

I smoothed my dress and put the *netella* on my shoulders in the traditional symbol of respect. I was ready.

As I walked toward the dining room, I could hear our sons' voices blending as they teased one another. I stood in the doorway for a moment, watching the three boys in front of me, and suddenly I felt very lonesome for Sammy, who was a junior in college in the States. Twenty-one-year-old Mickey

9

looked up and smiled. Bete' (age 14) and Lali (almost 9) saw me then, too, and their greetings brought our steward from the kitchen. Assafa bowed from the waist. *"Tenaystelegne,"* he said. "May God grant you health."

I sipped coffee as Bete' and Lali hastily finished their breakfast in order to run next door for a visit with their grandfather. Lali threw his little arms around my waist before skipping out the door. Bete' no longer had to stand on tiptoe to kiss me goodbye. Only slender, thoughtful Mickey—a young man now—remained in the dining room, his eyes following Assafa as the steward went back into the kitchen and closed the door behind him. His voice low, Mickey spoke.

"Mother, I heard you and Dad talking. If the Committee is a danger, why doesn't His Majesty stop them?"

I was concerned. If Mickey had heard us, perhaps others had too? Deme and I would have to be more careful. Already many of the cabinet members had been arrested and the Committee was encouraging citizens to spy on one another. I also spoke in a hushed tone.

"Son, I'm afraid His Majesty just doesn't see the danger. That's why I want to talk to him."

Mickey leaned down. "Then you think His Majesty will listen to you?"

I could only shrug my shoulders. Mickey stooped to hold my raincoat for me and wished me Godspeed.

Alone, I stepped onto the veranda into air so fresh I could almost taste it. The sweet, pungent fragrance of the eucalyptus trees was the hallmark of our mile-high city. I looked toward the distant mountains. The poison of the Committee could not spoil everything in this ancient city. I looked past the rose garden and hurried to my car parked at the bottom of the veranda steps.

At the entrance of the compound the attendant swung the iron gate open for me. I turned left onto the asphalt road that would take me into Addis Ababa.

The rain had stopped and the sun was trying to shine on the green mountains around the city. Lining the road were the eucalyptus trees, which stood like soldiers. But that morning the comparison made me uneasy since the military was rapidly falling under the control of the Committee.

As I rounded the first curve, that awful, all-too-symbolic factory with its huge sign displaying hammer and sickle came into view. Why had Ethiopia, the oldest Christian nation in Africa, allowed such Communist influence to pervade her capital? The Marxists had come pointing to the very real problems our country faced. Social inequality. Famine. Inflation. Strikes. Student rebellion. Mutiny in the military. Gently at first, and then more and more stridently, the Marxists blamed the government for these problems. When the mysterious Committee emerged out of unrest in the army, its members immediately began to step up the accusations.

How long would it be, I wondered, before the Committee began to attack even His Majesty? Perhaps hurt him! That's what I feared as I drove toward the palace on that July day. At least I'd try to warn him!

But what chance was there, I thought again, that the Father of Africa would listen to me? After all, I was just the daughter of poor missionary helpers whom His Majesty and Her Majesty had befriended years ago.

Just beyond the factory was a scene that reminded me of my childhood. I slowed the car as I passed a mule being urged along by a ragged farmer. On top of burlap bags on the mule's back sat a little girl of about seven. She turned to stare at my car. How often in my childhood had I perched on the back of a mule. And now I was driving a Mercedes on my way to visit His Majesty.

I turned toward the Jubilee Palace, which sat out of sight far across the grounds behind the tall wrought-iron fence. Guards in khaki stood at the main gate beneath twin stone lions set on pillars, symbols of Ethiopia. Those gates were used only for official ceremonies. For ordinary purposes, you entered the grounds by one of the side gates. The guards there recognized me and stood aside.

Just as I was about to drive through, a blue Volkswagen

11

parked near an evergreen tree caught my attention. The driver was staring at me. My hands tightened on the steering wheel. What was the matter with me? Was the atmosphere within my country so bad that I thought every man parked by the roadside was an informer for the Committee? Sadly I drove through and on toward the palace.

On both sides of the drive were enormous evergreen trees, their branches forming graceful tents over the rose beds. At the last bend, the palace porch with its four massive columns came into view. On top of the porch roof were two more stone lions and the pole displaying the green, yellow, and red national flag. I parked my car in one of the lots and then walked toward the palace, my eyes still on our beautiful flag as it caught the wind and billowed out again.

As I approached the front doors of the Jubilee Palace, two young men in white uniforms opened them from inside. I entered and bowed slightly as I greeted the aide-de-camp. He returned my bow as he spoke. *"Tenaystelegne,* may God grant you health."

"And may God grant you health," I answered.

Greetings in Ethiopia are ritualized, so I knew I would be asked about my family. I assured the aide that my four sons were all well, too, that my husband, Deme, was busy with our business in Dire Dawa, and that my father was in good health. Only then was I escorted down the long hallway to His Majesty's office. How many times had I walked over that beautiful carpet toward that open door? As I approached, I knew I would again be using the low bow my mother had taught me when I was a child.

The aide remained in the hall as His Majesty looked up and motioned for me to enter. Immediately I dropped into the low, difficult bow mastered so many years ago. When His Majesty invited me to stand, I noticed how prominent the veins were in his olive-skinned hands and that his beard had more gray in it than I remembered. He smiled, yet he seemed weary.

"Marta, are you well?"

"Yes, Your Majesty." As I started to inquire about his health, his words rolled over mine.

"Good. You must always guard your health, Marta." He seemed thin to me. "There is nothing so important. What brought you here today?"

I knew my time with him was limited. I had to get to my mission immediately.

"Your Majesty, I am much concerned. What do you think is happening in our country?"

He began to pace, his hands clasped behind his back. "Yes, the famine is severe. We need more roads, we need helicopters. But you know our needs, you know the burden we carry."

How tired he seemed! But I had to press on. I began to pace with him.

"Yes, Your Majesty. But this famine is being used by the Committee for their own ends. They're putting the blame on your government."

His Majesty turned suddenly. "Who has control over the weather? We do not believe such talk. Perhaps you dramatize."

My heart sank. "Forgive me, Your Majesty, but you are being blamed! The Committee pretends to want good for the country, but they don't stand for what they say."

"Oh, Marta. The Committee aren't Mussolini's Fascists— they are our own children. We educated them. We provided their jobs. This is just a bad time for all—the famine, the strikes, the inflation have all made everyone uneasy."

I refused to give in. "Your Majesty, Marxists are behind the student protests. I've talked to the students and I know. Marxists are behind the Committee, too."

His Majesty said nothing. Perhaps he did know. Perhaps this, at last, was my moment to speak.

"If you were, Your Majesty . . . if you were to form a government in exile . . . ."

13

He stopped pacing to smile at me patiently. "Marta, surely you aren't serious."

"I am most serious, Your Majesty. If you formed a government in exile, the people would have to make a choice. But if you don't leave, the Committee will soon take over and there will be only one government, and the world will accept the new one."

His Majesty began to walk around the office again. I pressed on. "It grieves me to think of what's ahead, Your Majesty. Leave while you can. Let the world know this group is dangerous."

"Do you really believe that, Marta?" He gently shook his head.

"Yes, Your Majesty. With the Committee here, our country isn't safe. *You* aren't safe."

Slowly he brought his hands together to their familiar position in front of him, the delicate fingers forming a circle. His voice now was a mixture of amusement and patience. "What will they do? Arrest the emperor?"

There! He had spoken aloud the very fear that had been rising from my subconscious. Suddenly I knew that they would arrest His Majesty, but I also knew that I'd never be able to make him believe that. As he stood next to me, it seemed as if he were in a long, dark hall. I tried to warn him, but he only walked further away. His voice brought me back to the reality of his office.

"Marta, you are acting like a worrisome woman, are you not? You fret when there is no need. We have raised these men from their childhood; they won't harm their country, nor us."

He made that last statement so emphatically that I knew it was useless to talk any longer. My time was up. But he spoke again.

"Marta, make sure you take care of your health. You are part of our family. Thank you for coming to see us."

I wanted to run to him, clasp his hands, beg him to leave. I respected this man and all that he stood for—the continuity of our country's long history, his symbolism of biblical heritage, his high Christian standards, his love for our people. But in the end all I could do was bow and back out of the room, knowing that although I had tried, there was no way for me or for anyone else to change what was happening.

The aide didn't speak as he escorted me back down the hallway. Was my disappointment so evident that he didn't dare look at me? The knot in my stomach turned to pain. I had tried and failed!

Outside the palace, I turned one last time to look up at the Ethiopian flag. In that moment, I realized that this was the last time I would visit His Majesty's office. This had been my final private meeting with that one whom I so greatly admired. A great sob welled up inside me.

At the gate, I looked for the blue Volkswagen, but it wasn't there. See, I told myself, it's just the atmosphere of the country right now—it's affecting you, too. That driver was probably just waiting for a friend. Things aren't as bad as you imagined.

But I knew that was wishful thinking. I'd had a glimpse of the future there in His Majesty's office. I knew I wasn't just being a worrisome, hysterical woman. Worse times were ahead for us all.

And where would our family fit into this fearful picture? What would become of Deme and me, and Father and the boys? The Committee was making new arrests every day. Would they come for us, too?

As I drove home that rainy morning, a scene from my youth passed through my mind. I was in my teens, visiting the missionary who had recently helped me make my commitment to the Lord and who was now teaching me what that decision meant.

At the time, I recall, my family and I were facing still one more economic crisis. "How good that you are a Christian right now," my teacher said.

At first I thought he meant the Lord would find money for us. I knew that God could do that perfectly well! But my teacher meant a different kind of protection. "I can't promise that He will keep you *from* the storm, Marta; but I can promise that He will keep you *in* the storm. You will be sheltered by the King."

I've never forgotten those words. I've held onto them ever since; their rhythm has become a part of my being.

I wondered now, as I drove away from the Jubilee Palace, how often my family and I would need this gift of His protecting presence during the days to come. I said the seven words over and over to myself that morning:

"You will be sheltered by the King."

Chapter Two

About 1924 four Swedish missionaries, with their pack mules and Ethiopian helpers, left the lush highlands of the Addis Ababa area for the western province of Welega to build a mission station.

Among the poor helpers who came with them were two Ethiopian Christians, a girl who served in the mission director's kitchen and a young man who helped with the mules. Although these young people were of different tribes, their mutual faith drew them together; they married and had three children, two sons and a daughter. The daughter was named Marta, which means "servant." I am that daughter.

My parents planned to stay in Welega, but the Fascist invasion changed everything. I remember being awakened by my trembling mother. We stood in the yard watching our house burn, sobbing as orange flames licked the black sky.

Our home gone, Mother took my brothers and me back to the highlands capital, Addis Ababa, while Father was forced underground and became a refugee in his own country. It would be years before he could join us.

I was amazed at the city of Addis. Mules and donkeys plodded through the narrow lanes between adobe houses. Dirty children played by open, garbage-filled ditches, and beggars crowded the streets.

Our home there was no better than anyone else's. But we had one big advantage. Mother was a dream-builder. She kept reminding me that my name meant servant, and that for a follower of Jesus Christ this was the most favored of all positions. "Being a servant is an attitude of heart," Mother often said as she planted in my mind the hope that I would get an

17

education—not for the sake of learning but so that I could serve my country.

This was an unusual dream in those days, since for most teenage girls a good marriage (arranged by her parents, of course) was the accepted goal. My parents had that marriage hope for me, but to it they added the aim of an education. The place to start, they agreed, was in a mission school.

I was happy at the school my parents chose, especially when my class was studying about our country. The textbook said we Ethiopians were descended from the Kemants and from the Cushites, a tribe fathered by the grandson of Noah. My favorite legend was the story of Solomon and the Queen of Sheba (Sheba is the ancient name for Ethiopia). A son, Menelik, was born to Solomon and the queen. When Menelik reached adolescence he was sent to his father Solomon, in the royal court in Jerusalem. Menelik eventually returned to Ethiopia to become Menelik I, the first emperor of the Solomonic dynasty. The man our books called His Imperial Majesty Haile Selassie I was the 225th emperor in that line.

As I studied I was impressed with all that His Majesty began to do to bring us out of the Dark Ages. He eliminated the feudal system; he outlawed the age-old practice of slavery; he began to rebuild our capital, bringing in modern sanitation and education; he tried desperately to reverse the killing cycle of famine.

But it was the spiritual heritage of Ethiopia that especially intrigued me. I began to see that when we bowed to His Majesty we were bowing not just to a person but to the biblical history of God working in the life of our nation. Tradition also told us that it was the eunuch instructed by Philip who brought Christianity to our land (Acts 8:26-39).

I was sorry to have my elementary school years come to an end when I was in my early teens, but I was excited about a new nursing program into which I was accepted. I liked what I learned in the classroom, which promised help for my countrymen, so often suffering from disease. But I didn't like having to clean instruments after surgery and I preferred ward duties to washing walls and floors. "Never mind," my mother reminded me. "Other kinds of servanthood will follow."

One day three of us were assigned to scrub the lobby walls of the hospital. I had just put down my bucket when a black car pulled up in front of the main entrance. An aide jumped out, opened the back door of the car, and then with lowered head held out his hand.

Suddenly into the lobby rushed two of the nurses calling, "His Majesty and Her Majesty are here! Hurry!" They grabbed our buckets and scrub brushes. They managed to get everything stowed into a corner as the aide was opening the front door. I stood awed in the middle of the lobby. I was going to be in the same room with His Majesty! I strained to see the faces of the regal pair as they walked up the asphalt path toward the open door, but the nurse behind me grabbed my arm.

"Marta! Bow!"

Bow? Oh, dear. I had practiced that difficult bow as all Ethiopian children were taught to do, but I certainly hadn't expected to use it so soon. Quickly I joined the girls along the right wall just as His Majesty stepped into the lobby. My bow was flawless—legs folded beneath me, back parallel to the floor, head a few inches from the tiles.

His Majesty paused for only a moment and then spoke to the head nurse.

"Are these your new students?"

"Yes, Your Majesty." That was the signal for us to step forward.

His Majesty approached me first. "And what is your name?" he asked in a kind, fatherly manner.

I kept my eyes properly downcast as I answered. "Marta, Your Majesty."

"Are you studying well, Marta?"

I was astounded that His Majesty was carrying on a conversation with me. Out of the corner of my eye I could see that Her Majesty was standing next to us now, her round, patient eyes smiling at me. The aide was standing behind them both, listening. I suddenly felt too tall next to His Majesty.

"Yes, Your Majesty. But there is much for me to learn."

"And what have you learned to do best, Marta?"

"I'm very good at washing walls, Your Majesty."

I certainly wasn't trying to be amusing, but His Majesty chuckled and turned to his wife. "Did you hear what she said? Perhaps we should inspect these walls."

And so it was that a casual comment began an almost Cinderella-like relationship between me, the daughter of two poor missionary helpers, and the emperor. His Majesty made frequent visits to the hospital since his people's health was high in his order of priorities.

When His Majesty and Her Majesty came for one of their tours, we students followed them through the wards. His Majesty remembered my comment about the walls and always asked about my progress. Whenever it seemed appropriate, I gave him a real answer instead of one that was merely polite.

It was shortly after I began the nursing program that I discovered I was too squeamish to give shots or perform some of the other nursing duties. Regrettably I left the hospital program and went back to an academic school. Soon afterward, my parents decided I should be married. After all, I was already 15 years old. My husband to be was Peter Myhre, a Norwegian who had come to Ethiopia as a missionary and who was now working in the Ministry of Education.

Peter was 52 years old, and I knew him slightly through my parents' missionary association. I certainly had never suspected he was interested in marrying me. He had followed the Ethiopian way of not speaking to the girl, but going to her parents for permission. He also stated his intention of taking me to the United States so I could get the education I wanted.

My parents accepted for me, and Peter and I were married at the end of term.

Shortly after our marriage I went back to school. By the time that next term ended, I was expecting my first child.

As the baby began to develop, I occasionally wondered how I would ever be able to bow if I saw His Majesty, but I dismissed the worry since I doubted that our paths were likely to cross. But I was wrong, as I discovered when I was about eight months pregnant.

I had done well in school, receiving the second-highest grades in my class. The honor pleased me for a special reason. Each year the three top students from every class of every school received awards at the palace itself! Their Majesties, everybody knew, sat next to each other in the throne room, and students filed into their royal presence in two lines—His Majesty receiving the boys, Her Majesty the girls. I had earned the right to take part in that ceremony! But the day before the awards were supposed to be given, I was asked to report to the Education Office. Mr. Atjar smoothed his shirt over his huge stomach, which was about as noticeable as mine. He seemed nervous, but came right to the point.

"We're pleased with your grades. But of course you can't join the others for the ceremony tomorrow, under the circumstances."

I couldn't believe I was hearing him correctly. How did he dare say I couldn't receive what I had earned? I was careful to keep the fury out of my voice.

"Under what circumstances, sir?"

"Well, you see—uh—we are afraid that people will misunderstand."

Ah, I was beginning to realize what he was talking about. But I was going to make him say it.

"Misunderstand *what*, sir?"

Again he cleared his throat. "Well, uh—you see, there has been talk about the two girls who became pregnant at the government boarding school . . . now here *you* are. We just can't have you lined up with our other students tomorrow."

"But I'm married. You know that."

"Yes, but that's just it. There are no other married students in the country. You are the only one. To have you march with the others tomorrow is unheard of. But of course we will still see that you receive your award. It will be sent to you."

He seemed to expect the conversation to end there. But I refused to give up what I had earned. An odd stubborn streak replaced my politeness.

"No. I am a married student. I earned the award. I will go."

"But you can't do that. People will misunderstand."

"I *will* go. And they will give me the award. People will just have to understand that there is such a possibility, that married women can go to school."

He was close to wailing. "But you are *eight* months pregnant!"

"And I have been married *ten* months. I will not stay home."

The next morning the students lined up at the school early for the mile-long walk to the palace. I arrived extra early and took my place, my shoulders squared defiantly. I tried to pull in my tummy. I chuckled at the futility; I wouldn't give a perfect bow today.

When Mr. Atjar arrived he ignored me. I knew I had won, after all.

The walk was leisurely and I enjoyed the contrast of the white buildings and the fragrant green of the eucalyptus trees. How good it would be to see His Majesty and Her Majesty again, although I was certain they'd never remember me.

At the palace, we straightened the two lines—boys in one, girls in the other—before quietly filing onto the marble porch with its massive columns. I looked at the stone lions in awe. Was I really about to see the throne room?

Uniformed guards stood at their posts as we started down the long hallway. I marveled at the thick Persian rugs under my feet and strained to see the door to the throne room ahead of us. At last we were there.

I caught my breath at the scene before me. Red velvet curtains hung at the windows behind two gilded thrones. The royal pair sat stiffly at the end of the room. Her Majesty wore a simple white dress that reached to her ankles—much like the dresses the Amhara country women wore on festival days. She had her cape on, too. His Majesty was wearing his tan military uniform. I thought how small he looked in that large chair, but immediately I scolded myself for such a disrespectful thought.

His Majesty nodded slightly, and the line moved forward slowly as the aide read the name of each student to receive an award. I moved with the line, but still kept my eyes on the royal couple.

There was only one student left in front of me when I glanced toward His Majesty just as he looked toward the girls' line. He smiled.

"You're going to have a baby!"

I had time only to answer, "Yes, Your Majesty," and return his smile, before my name was announced. I bowed as low as I could and then accepted the book that Her Majesty held out to me. As I thanked her, she clasped my hands in hers and said, "Marta, we are so glad to see you again. How happy we are for your award . . . and for your baby."

Oh, they did remember! There was special clapping for me as I received the award. People were saying it was all right for our women to go to school after they married! I especially liked that. My stubbornness had a good side to it after all.

After our son was born a few weeks later, both His Majesty and Her Majesty visited us in the hospital.

As I pulled back the mosquito netting from the bassinet near my bed, Her Majesty smiled. "Oh, what a beautiful child! What have you named him?"

"Samuel, Your Majesty."

She nodded, still smiling at the baby. As the three of us looked at the tiny sleeping form, we were suddenly no longer royal couple and schoolgirl, but parents marveling at the miracle of another precious life.

His Majesty interrupted my thought. "Now we suppose you will not be returning to your studies?"

"Oh, no, Your Majesty. I must go back to school. I will be gone for just a few hours each day and my mother will help take care of Sammy."

He seemed surprised, but he still smiled. "You are a strong girl, Marta."

Strong. I liked that word better than "stubborn."

Sammy was less than a year old when I began to see that we were never going to the United States as Peter had planned.

One day a truck stopped in front of our modest home in Addis Ababa. The driver and his assistant greeted me but asked for the household helper. She was a woman who had cooked for Peter for years and she seemed to know why the men were there. She immediately directed them into the dining room, and they carried the table and chairs out of the house and onto their truck.

After they had left, she cleaned the room thoroughly but said nothing to me. I thought we were going to get a new dining set that would be delivered the next day while I was in school. But when I came home, there was no new set waiting. Nor the next day—nor the next.

Finally I approached our helper. "Aren't we getting new furniture?"

She seemed surprised at my question but answered with a simple, "No."

"But where is the other set? Why did they take it away?"

"Oh, that one belonged to the mission. They were just storing it here until they needed it. Another missionary has arrived, so they took it to him."

I said no more, but I started to pay closer attention to what

24

was happening around me. Little by little I began to realize just how things were in our home. Our house was rented; I had thought we owned it. By the time our second son, Mickey, was born, I was discovering that we were deep in debt. Peter had a good salary and we had a cook, but I hadn't known that he owned nothing because he gave his salary away to help other people. And when his salary money ran out, he borrowed enormous sums on his good name. He was personally paying the school bills for dozens of children.

Peter was so interested in helping others that he didn't even notice what he wore each day. He had one suit and one pair of trousers—both very short and worn. His thinking was beyond this world while mine was on the security I wanted for my sons, Sammy and Mickey.

Added to my concern about our finances was my knowledge that there was a real possibility I would be a widow within just a few years. Peter was in his mid-fifties now and was suffering from a duodenal ulcer. In the morning, I would watch him drink a glass of buttermilk, and I knew that that was all he would have until his dinner of two boiled eggs. So, realizing that I might well become a widow soon, I was even more determined to get a good education in order to be able to support Sammy and Mickey.

But just as I told myself that the dream of going to school in America would have to wait, my mother intervened. She insisted that I go, pointing out that although four years seemed an impossibly long time to be away from my family, it wasn't as if the boys would be left alone. She'd take care of them. After all, she pointed out, it was the custom in Ethiopia for grandmothers to help raise the children.

Peter was enthusiastic about the idea, and we began making inquiries about schools, visas, cram courses in English, work-study programs in America. The day finally arrived when everything was in order. On a chilly morning in August 1953, the entire family saw me off.

"How pretty you look, Marta," Mother said in the waiting

25

lounge at the airport. She reached up and dabbed at my eyes with her handkerchief. "Don't be so sad. The boys will be just fine."

Sammy, almost two now, and Mickey, a year younger, looked at me solemnly from their grandmother's lap. I hugged them both, determined not to cry.

I anticipated being away for four years, during which time I was determined to complete my high school and undergraduate work. But when Peter's numerous projects later caused him to stop sending me money, I had to increase my work schedule as a nurse's aide and couldn't take a full load of classes each semester. As a result, I was away from my family even longer than four years.

Often, at school, I thought about returning home. When I did come back I knew I'd find many, many changes, and I wondered what they would be.

Chapter 3

June 8, 1958

I peered out the airplane window, trying to see through the clouds beyond the wing. How much longer before the mountains around Addis Ababa would appear? How much longer before I could hug my family? Would Sammy and Mickey recognize me?

I had been in the States for five years! Thoughts of my sons, my parents, Peter, His Majesty, all bumped against one another. I thought of my father with his work on the coffee plantation in another province, and of my mother's dream of my education, finally realized. And I wondered what Addis Ababa was going to be like now.

Mother had written in her frequent letters that new buildings and roads were being built everywhere. What an exciting time to be coming back to Ethiopia! I thought of the promise I had written in the front of my Bible while I was in the States—"I will return and will serve Him by doing good to my people." And that's exactly what I planned.

At last my jewel city began to appear below us as the plane started its descent. "Thank You, Lord," I whispered as we touched down, and I strained to see who was waiting at the gate for me. I saw Mother first, and then Mickey, five-and-a-half, and Sammy, seven. Behind them was my childhood friend Gera. But Peter wasn't with them. . . .

As soon as the plane door was opened, I was out of my seat and down the ramp. Sammy recognized me immediately and waved enthusiastically while Mother stooped to put her arm around Mickey and point me out to him. How beautiful his grin was when he finally saw me! I wanted to hurry to them, but the customs guard was asking the usual mundane questions and expecting my full attention.

At last I was dismissed and I ran with my arms outstretched toward my young sons. Both of them raced toward me, calling, "Mommy! Mommy!" I marveled that Mickey had outgrown his baby chubbiness and was almost as tall as his brother. Suddenly their arms were around my waist and I dropped to my knees to hug them, crying with happiness.

Mother and my friend Gera hugged the three of us and both talked at once, but somehow I managed to ask about Peter. Mother's joy faded.

"You must be ready for a change in him, Marta," she said. "He's aged and he isn't well. His heart is still in the field. He's at a school in the north but will be back Thursday."

I was disappointed that he wasn't there and that his habits hadn't altered while I had been away. But Peter was always going to be Peter, and I needn't hope for him to be different.

Well, Lord, I said inwardly as we headed home in Gera's car, *You have given me two special little boys from my marriage.* I put my arms around them both, and they snuggled closer to me. *I want to thank You.*

"What do you make of our city?" Mother asked, interrupting my thoughts. She and Sammy and Mickey excitedly pointed out the many new buildings. Most of the open, garbage-filled ditches were gone. Many of the narrow roads were now wide avenues carrying streams of cars. I suspected these were the smallest of changes I'd soon be encountering.

My parents' home was in the old part of town. Mother had planted several rosebushes at the corners of the adobe house, and Mickey and Sammy pulled me from bush to bush to show me each beautiful bloom. At the back of the house was the vegetable garden that the boys had helped their grandmother plant. I'd worried that it might take days for Mickey and Sammy to feel comfortable with me. But every single night while I was away Mother had shown them my picture and had reminded them of my love. As soon as she knew when I'd be

28

coming home she had begun counting the days with them, making their anticipation grow.

A few days later Peter came home. He'd aged more than I had expected. His skin had a yellow cast and his once sandy hair was totally gray. He needed rest, but he waved aside my plea to postpone his next trip. He said he would relax a bit when he finished his current project. I shook my head, knowing he would always have just one more project.

I was not surprised when Peter left that same afternoon for an eastern province. He still drove himself. He was fired by a passion to educate his adopted people. It didn't come as a surprise, either, when the message came that my Peter—my unusual, exasperating, wonderful Peter—had collapsed in a distant province. He died there before I could get to him. He died as he had lived, alone among the people he wanted to help. He should not have been alone that way. But Peter never did follow the paths of ordinary men.

Peter, whom I hardly knew, left an unaccountable void in my life. I realized after his death that I would never again meet someone like him, and that realization was worth treasuring. I received comfort from the message of sympathy from His Majesty and Her Majesty. Hundreds of my countrymen came to his funeral. I marveled at the number of lives he had touched during his more than 30 years of service to Ethiopia.

In our culture there is a 40-day mourning period in which a family receives guests who wish to offer condolences. For several days after Peter's funeral, family members and friends, government officials and former students visited us to say how profoundly Peter had influenced their lives.

For seven days friends and family sat with me in the living room of my mother's home. Occasionally Mickey and Sammy joined me, looking very young and fatherless in their new size eight suits. Always Mother and Gera sat with me, too.

Shortly after this time one of my friends told me Demeke

29

Tekle-Wold had asked about me. I stammered my thanks as I hastily explained that Deme had been one of my classmates back in the States. Actually we had been good friends, and the memory of his dark, penetrating eyes and fine, long nose lingered in my mind. But I didn't want to think about him. There was room in my thoughts right now only for my grief and worry about my sons' future.

In the weeks following the funeral there were many details to attend to. I discovered, for one thing, how very deep in debt we were. There were outstanding accounts for groceries, clothing, and school expenses for the students Peter had sponsored. I badly needed a job, not only to support my family but also to pay off these debts.

It was customary for college students returning from abroad to begin work almost immediately in one of the many government ministries. When I wrote to His Majesty to thank him for his words of sympathy, I added that I was looking forward to doing my part for my country.

One afternoon Gera helped me vacate and close Peter's rented house so that I could move back to my parents' home, where my sons and I would live.

"What will you do now, Marta? I don't suppose you'd want to go into business with me?" Gera owned a restaurant in Addis. But that was not at all what I had in mind.

"As soon as the mourning period is over," I said, "I'll accept whatever job His Majesty offers me."

"What will you do personally? Of course you'll marry again."

I looked at her in surprise. "Marry? Gera! I've just buried one husband and already you are planning my second marriage?"

Gera shrugged. "Well, remember you're back in Ethiopia now. You are expected to remarry. And soon, too."

I shook my head. "Not me, Gera. I don't want to be rude, but that's that."

In spite of myself, however, I found that I was remembering

Deme Tekle-Wold. There had been very few Ethiopian students at Highlands University, so it had been a delight to meet someone from home. Deme and I spontaneously greeted one another in Amharic when we met for the first time on the campus during my second year in the States. It was a wonder how often Deme happened to be coming out of his dormitory as I walked by.

Since I was married, I had no thought of dating and I was happy just to talk with someone from home. When we were together we were always in a group, never talking about personal matters, and so I didn't mention my husband or my sons.

One night we were all having a snack at the coffee shop. Others were in deep discussion about a math problem. Deme listened for a moment, then turned to me. His quiet voice was unusually soft.

"What are you going to do when you graduate, Marta?"

"I suppose I'll get a job in government. What will you do?"

"Someday I want to have my own business. I . . . ."

Deme glanced at me and I saw that his eyes were most serious. "I like to think of you as an important part of that future, Marta."

I stared at him, feeling very stupid. I was married and yet I had never been courted. I hadn't recognized the tone of his voice when he spoke to me. I had not properly translated the smile in his eyes. Why hadn't I adopted the American habit of wearing a wedding band! While I was trying to find some way to apologize to Deme, he spoke again.

"Before I came to the States, Marta, I prayed that the Lord would show me my future wife. The one He had chosen for me. That first day that you and I met, I heard an inner voice saying, *This is your wife*. Being in His will is very important to me, Marta; but falling in love with you has been easy."

I covered my face with my left hand and motioned feebly with my right for him to stop.

"Deme, forgive me. I didn't realize what was happening."

31

Why was this so difficult? "But I already have a husband back home and two little sons. Oh, Deme, I should have told you right away. But I never thought . . . ."

Finally Deme broke the miserable silence. "Who is your husband?"

"Peter Myhre, in the Ministry of Education."

Dully he answered. "Yes. I've heard of him."

In the long moments that followed, neither of us spoke. I felt utterly wretched to think I hadn't realized something like this might happen. Thankfully, the math discussion our friends were having was soon over, and we all left together. Within a month Deme transferred to Washington State.

The thing I missed most after Deme left was his Christian outlook. Deme's life, too, was centered in the Lord. There was an innocence about him that I found in none of my other classmates. Some of the students—to be honest, even some of the Ethiopians there—frightened me with their "me-first" views. But not Deme. He spoke refreshingly of his idealism. He encouraged me to keep up my prayer life and he talked about Jesus Christ as naturally as he talked about college friends.

After Deme transferred to Washington State he wrote a chatty letter describing the school and the surrounding mountains that reminded him of home. At the end of the letter, he said he wanted us to remain friends and that he was sorry for the embarrassment he had caused me.

Now, here in Addis Ababa, I was faced with the task of having to make a living. After the traditional days of mourning, I accepted the position of liaison officer for the Point Four educational program.

Almost immediately, however, the welcome routine of life disappeared. In its place came the hint that something was deeply wrong in our country. The first glimpse of the poison that was even then working away at our inward parts came to me almost before I had settled into my new job.

32

Every morning I arose early, saw the boys off to elementary school, then left for my office near the palace. I did my best to be cheerful. And there was much to be cheerful about. The drive from my parents' modest home into the new part of the city delighted me, as I loved seeing the green mountains ringing our mile-high capital. I had a good job. My mother and sons were well and my father was happy with his work on the coffee plantation. I was back in my homeland, beginning the life of service my mother had spoken about so often.

Much was new in Addis, but some things about human nature never change, as I was soon to find out. I had been at my job with the Point Four program almost a month when I was called to the palace.

In the throne room I bowed the low traditional bow, and then exchanged formal greetings with the dignified ruler who had first spoken to me years ago about scrubbing hospital walls. But today His Majesty, standing in front of his gilded throne, didn't mention that long-ago activity, and he seemed to be in a hurry.

"Marta," said His Majesty, "we are putting you in Foreign Affairs because of the rumors we hear of corruption in that department. And we expect you to stop it."

Corruption! What was he talking about? I wanted to ask for more details but I was on the verge of being dismissed.

His final statements were just as confusing to me as his first. "You will be in the Passport Department. If you have any problem, we want you to report to us directly. It's because we consider you one of the family."

What an astonishing way to speak of the trust he had in me! Ever since His Majesty and Her Majesty had first met me in the hospital, the royal family had taken what seemed to me a special interest in my life. They had sent silver cups to us when Sammy and Mickey were born. They had carefully followed my career in the States, offering financial help at crucial moments. They'd sent greetings on my return and personal condolences upon Peter's death. I wondered how

33

many hundreds of other young people this couple was encouraging.

An aide appeared at the door to escort me out. His Majesty had told me as much as he felt necessary.

The next day I visited the minister of Foreign Affairs to tell him how happy I was to be part of his office. I also wanted to know about this corruption in the Passport Department. Widespread bribery, the minister told me, had become a pattern within the department. I'm afraid I was scandalized. As I left his office that morning I realized that my idealism had suffered still another blow.

It was Mother who brought me back to a right perspective.

"Marta," Mother said, "you should never idealize another human. Our very nature is sinful. The only person you can idealize is God. Let Him be your example!"

It was after this conversation with Mother that I began to analyze the conditions that led to bribery in the Passport Department. In order to speak to anyone in authority, people first had to make appointments with a stepladder series of assistants. Each rung was vulnerable to bribery. I could stop this by eliminating the middleman, so my first order was that all requests for interviews in my department had to be made to me directly.

Because of this decision to eliminate the chain of command within my department, my appointment book was so filled that I had to do my paperwork at home.

One night Sammy and Mickey were playing with their building blocks while I worked. Someone knocked at the door. I had to step over the boys to get to the door. There stood Deme with two packages under his arm.

"*Tenaystelegne*, Marta."

I stammered a greeting but continued to stand in the doorway, trying to figure out why he had come. Deme smiled as if reading my thoughts.

"Are your sons well?" he asked.

"Why, yes." I decided to ask him to come in. As I introduced

34

seven-year-old Sammy, and Mickey, who was going on six, they bowed from the waist as Ethiopian children are taught, but their eyes remained on the two brightly wrapped packages under his arm.

Deme held out the presents. "When I saw these, I thought of two little boys who might like them."

Immediately Mickey and Sammy tore off the paper and each discovered a toy truck, identical except for color. Barely remembering to thank him in their excitement, they started pushing the trucks along imaginary roads.

Deme sat down in a chair while I returned to the sofa. We talked about our jobs and about the changes we had seen since our return. Finally there was a silence and we both watched the boys playing. Then Deme leaned forward.

"Marta, this is awkward for me since I don't want to appear happy about your husband's death. But I haven't changed my mind in these years. I'm still in love with you and I want to marry you."

My thoughts went back to the coffee shop in the States where I had told Deme about Peter and the boys. This time I wanted to choose my words carefully.

"Deme, you are kind, but I couldn't marry again. Look at these files! For the next year or so I'll have to spend 100 percent of my energy on my career. It would be unfair to any man to come into the middle of this."

Deme nodded. "I'll just have to be patient," he said.

Before I could answer he was down on the floor with Sammy and Mickey and was stacking the blocks into ramps. Even though I started working on my papers again, my eyes strayed to the laughing threesome. I shook my head. Deme would grow tired of waiting.

During the next several months Deme and I occasionally met at government offices or he stopped by our house. At the end of each visit he routinely asked me to marry him. Just as routinely I reminded him of my many responsibilities. His penetrating eyes would study me before he added, "Please think about it, Marta."

Our conversations often centered on our jobs. "It frustrates me," I once blurted out, "that there is bribery in our government."

Deme nodded. "The only perfect place is the Lord's Kingdom," he said. "Until that comes fully, you must do what you can in the place where He has put you."

He didn't dwell on his statement, but that night I had much to ponder.

I hadn't allowed myself to think of remarrying, but I found Deme increasingly on my mind. He had a happy relationship with my sons, and he shared my faith in the Lord. In short, Deme worked his way into my heart, even though I had determined that this would not happen.

So it was that one day when Deme asked me again to marry him, I startled him by replying, "I will think about it." He lost no time in making plans, and we were married on January 31, 1959.

Chapter Four

The next hint that there was trouble in our land came when I discovered by accident that His Majesty's directives were being ignored by his staff.

Even though Deme was doing well as head of a vocational school, His Majesty knew that neither of us had worked long enough to afford a house. In typical fashion, he did something about it. He gave Sammy and Mickey a house to honor their late father's service to Ethiopia. It was a tan, plastered house, attractively landscaped with flowering shrubs, and we were all most appreciative.

For some reason, though, that house never seemed to belong to us. I always had the feeling that we were visiting and that I needed to capture moments there in my mind as if they wouldn't last.

One of these mental photographs was especially precious to me. The house was near a police school where trainees drilled. Almost every afternoon at five o'clock His Majesty took a walk toward the school. Sammy and Mickey always watched for their monarch, darting out from our yard to greet him the moment he appeared. His Majesty would take their hands and ask them questions about their day. Time after time as they walked toward the parade ground—the short, slightly built emperor and my two sons—one of the boys would grip His Majesty's little finger!

There was another reason for my sense that a shadow lay over that house.

The title was never delivered.

His Majesty ordered the transfer, but his order was ignored. I was surprised that a directive from the throne was not followed. The insult was a warning, to be sure. But it was also—

completely unknown to us at the time—an event that I believe later played a surprising role in our lives.

At first I thought I was making progress rooting out bribery in my department. But my success was superficial, as I discovered when I myself was indirectly offered a bribe.

Semien was a clever fellow. He never came right out with the bribe offer, so I had no grounds for a charge against him. The attempt came about, I now think, because people in government knew that Deme and I had no title to the house we were living in. They could see for themselves, too, that Deme and I lived simply. We were trying systematically to pay off Peter's debts. We were also investing all of our excess cash, primarily in real estate.

Anyone observing us would have seen only one luxury. We did decide to get help running the house. After much interviewing, Deme chose Assafa, a small man whose gentle nature impressed me immediately. His thin face was shiny and the whiteness of his work jacket contrasted with his dark complexion. Assafa's brown eyes were patient, like those of one who has learned it is useless to hurry.

With Assafa in charge of our house, I had a somewhat easier schedule. This was a good thing because I still had a constant battle keeping bribery out of my department. That fact disturbed me. The corruption that had settled over our land was so pernicious that if it was suppressed in one area, it appeared elsewhere. This I discovered personally when Semien began approaching me.

Several mornings a week Semien would stop by my desk, offering to help in any way he could. One day as he started to leave, he turned back as though he had just remembered something.

"Oh, know what I heard yesterday?"

I glanced at my watch. My first visitor was due in ten minutes. "What did you hear?"

"Tadesse is going to sell his house. You know, the big white one near the airport. I thought you should have his fine place."

I shook my head. "Me? We can't afford to buy a home now." Of course I didn't mention those awful debts that we were still paying off.

Semien seemed surprised. He put his hands on my desk, then leaned forward. He whispered, "But there are ways to work that out. Just go see the house."

His emphasis on the word *ways* let me know he was offering a bribe. I was so startled by his suggestion that I could only deny my interest again and busy myself with my papers.

Semien didn't give up. His hints continued, at least once a week. Each time he heard of a house for sale he stopped in to tell me about it, always hinting that there were ways. Just as regularly I would shake my head sternly and continue working.

When this had gone on for several months, I discovered that Deme and I were going to have a baby. One morning as I was smiling to myself about the little life silently developing, Semien appeared. This time he sighed sympathetically.

"Marta, you know it's not right for you to work so hard. Others don't do half as much as you do and yet they have new cars and two or three houses while you drive that old automobile and don't even have title to one house."

How did he know that!

But I merely glanced at him as he shook his head sadly and continued. "The trouble is, Marta, you just don't know how to make money."

My voice was firm. "No, I won't accept anything like that."

"Like *what*, Marta!" His voice had been soothing, but now he became bolder. "It wouldn't be a bribe! Some of my friends want to help you, that's all. It's no different from when His Majesty gives away cars or . . . or houses."

I still did not rise to the lure. I simply shook my head. "You tell your friends that I don't want them to do anything for me.

The cars His Majesty gives to people are in appreciation for service already given. Your offer is for service in the future. There *is* a difference."

He shrugged. "But Marta, think of having your own home."

At that moment, I felt the baby move for the first time. I smiled at Semien. "Oh, didn't I tell you? We *have* started building our home." And I smiled again as I thought of the baby who would be a symbol of the home Deme and I had established.

Semien was surprised. "A home? Where? When can I see it?"

"Oh, you'll see it when the time is right."

Semien left the office looking perplexed. As the weeks passed he kept asking about the progress of our home. "Oh, it's coming along fine," I always answered as I turned back to my appointment book. When Semien finally realized I was pregnant, he was all the more curious about our new home.

Meanwhile Deme and I were so excited about the arrival of our baby that we no longer worried about the absent title. There were happy dinners with relatives, and shopping trips to choose furniture and wallpaper for the nursery. Sammy and Mickey asked a myriad shy questions. I marveled at how much they had grown since I had returned from the States two years earlier.

As Deme and I planned for our baby, we couldn't decide on a name. But at last the day arrived, and a baby boy was born. What an exciting time it was! Mother and Sammy and Mickey, Gera, and dozens of relatives all came to visit us while Deme beamed his new-father smile.

His Majesty and Her Majesty came, too. They gave our new son a sterling silver cup, like the cups they had given to Sammy and Mickey at their births. Shortly after they left, Semien arrived.

We exchanged greetings and then I gestured toward the bassinet. "Remember what I said about our building a home?"

Semien was immediately interested. "Yes! You never let me see it."

I pulled back the baby's blanket. "Well, here you are. Come look. Here is my home."

As I said *bete'*, the Amharic word for "my home," Deme nodded. Such joy flooded me that I didn't mind Semien's glares. He found an excuse to leave. Deme and I bent over the blue-blanketed form in the bassinet and I whispered, "Bete'. Welcome, our own little Bete'."

Deme gripped my hand and I knew that we had found the name for our son.

The drift into trouble in our country became more pronounced. It took careful observation to see it, though. On the surface all was normal. His Majesty hosted elegant dinners to honor heads of state. Often on official tours I rode in the second car with the wife of the visiting dignitary while our important guests rode in the first car with His Majesty. Frequently during those tours I remembered my early years when I rode on the back of a mule.

Things were going well for us personally, too. Deme had made profitable investments in an export business and in a coffee plantation in the hot eastern lowlands. The boys were doing well. We delighted in our honey-complexioned little Bete' and in the accomplishments of Mickey and Sammy.

It was the accepted practice for people to send their children abroad on a government scholarship. But like the promised title for our house, scholarships for Mickey and Sammy never materialized. I fought the disappointment and budgeted for their school fees, not knowing that this was all part of the Lord's protection.

New signs emerged that behind-the-scenes changes were taking place. When Bete' was four years old I was abruptly transferred to a lesser job by my superior in order to make room for one of his friends. For the first time I began to see a new reality. Before that demotion I lived in a utopia, believing that my position was secure since His Majesty had appointed me. But obviously this was no longer true. Who was running our country, anyway?

One night at dinner, when I could finally talk about the bitterness I felt, Deme and I broke the news of my demotion to Mother. Mother spent most of her time these days reading the Bible, praying, and fasting. When I finished with my story she leaned forward, her arms on the table as she spoke.

"Marta, you can never be protected by men. Don't you remember what you were taught as a child? You can truly be guarded only by the King."

"Yes, Mother, but how can I deal with the bitterness I feel? How should I approach this new job?"

She closed her eyes before she answered and it occurred to me that she was praying.

"Don't think of what you have lost," Mother said at last. "Accept the new position as from the Lord. Don't think in terms of human justice. Be concerned instead for the biblical justice coming to our country. What are we doing for the desperate and the poor? What about our country's orphans? Are we continuing to fight corruption wherever we see it?"

It was a proper challenge, and I determined to use whatever influence I had, even in this new job, to battle these evils.

If it had not been for Mother's comments from time to time that we were headed for a crisis, all would have seemed normal and hopeful. In the midst of my new assignment I became pregnant again. Sammy and Mickey were at school in England, Bete' was almost six years old, and we were looking forward to having another baby in the house. Our son Lali was born in July 1965. He had Deme's strong jaw and my mother's beautiful eyes. Shortly after Lali arrived, we finally paid off the last of Peter's massive debts, and to celebrate we decided at last to build our own home.

We found a plot of land just outside Addis Ababa. At the

front of the property was a majestic fig tree and across the back, where we planned to build a house for my mother, ran a stream. Without hesitation, we bought the land and began to build our long-awaited home. It slowly took shape, a two-story house with wide steps leading onto the veranda, two kitchens—one for traditional Ethiopian open-hearth cooking and the other for European cuisine—and a formal dining room for the diplomatic dinners I knew we would soon be serving.

To crown our joy in the new home, I planted squares of roses, each plot containing a deeper shade of pink and red as they approached the house, until those near the veranda were crimson. The line of rosebushes with their crescendo of color could be seen from the master bedroom as well as from the veranda and the living room.

One thing marred our happiness as we moved into our new home. Mother's health declined because of advanced cancer, and we immediately moved her into our bedroom overlooking the roses. For the next two years she never left her bed, and she died in April 1968. The house seemed devastatingly empty after her death.

My father had been a shadow figure for all of these years, but upon Mother's death remorse gripped him. When I saw the white-bearded man I embraced him and gave way to the tears that I had tried to choke back. "Oh, Marta," he said. "I have missed so much. Can we try to make up for those lost years?" He moved into the little house by the stream, and we began to do just that.

Father couldn't spend enough time with his grandsons, and he suddenly became interested again in things of the Lord. This complete turnabout evidenced itself in his giving his life to fasting and prayer. Then, strangely, he took over Mother's role as he began to speak prophetically about the future of our beloved Ethiopia.

Several months after Mother's death, a rumor began to

spread through Addis Ababa that I was going to be appointed to the Senate! Ethiopia had never had a woman senator, so Deme and I dared not become too excited. Our Parliament contained two houses—the lower house where seats were won by popular election, and the Senate, the upper house, where seats were filled by appointment from the throne.

A few days after the rumor began going around, I was called to the palace and escorted to the office of the minister of pen. This time I was told of the appointment before I went into the throne room! "His Imperial Majesty has graciously consented," the minister of pen announced solemnly, "for you to be appointed as a senator."

Senator! What a nice sound! A few minutes later, as I bowed to His Majesty and heard the words from his lips, too, I thought again of my college promise to serve the Lord by serving my people. With tears of gratitude I whispered, "Thank You."

During my first months in Parliament, I remembered Mother's counsel and tried to work for change in three problem areas—the scourge of alcoholism; the desperation of our street beggars; the plight of our orphans; and the inheritance tax law. One by one my efforts at reform were shot down. I presented a bill limiting the sale of alcohol; it didn't pass. I formulated a bill designed to help beggars find work; the bill was tabled. I tried, both inside and outside the Senate, to increase aid to orphans; I received only token support.

Some of my fellow senators laughed at me. One was a fellow named Zelke who was famous for his four gold teeth that glistened as he talked.

"Marta, don't look so glum," he said after my Aid to Orphans bill was defeated. "You're taking this whole thing far too seriously. Enjoy your time in the Senate, but don't think you are going to make a difference. The trick is to appear busy and enjoy all the benefits."

44

I shook my head, trying not to stare at those incredible gold teeth. "No, Zelke. I have a promise to keep."

That night I shared my frustrations with Deme.

"Do what you can, Marta, and leave the results to God," Deme said.

It was advice that helped me greatly as I and other reform-minded senators faced defeat after defeat. But we wouldn't give up. Where we failed to bring about change through the law, we worked on our own, outside the government.

My duties with the orphanage where I tried to help out didn't stop with fund-raising; scrubbing floors and walls was just as important. The orphanage soon became a family project. Lali and Bete' would carry filthy mattresses to the rubbish heap while Deme unwrapped new ones. Often we spent our Saturdays at the orphanage, plunging our hands into buckets of soapy disinfectant.

On one such afternoon, I was scrubbing the lobby wall when the front door suddenly opened. I turned around just as His Majesty walked in with four aides.

I tried to cover my surprise with a quick bow, as His Majesty looked at my water-splashed clothing and then at the bucket near my feet. He brought his hands together in front of his chest and smiled.

"Ah, our dear Marta. We see after all of these years, you are still washing walls."

Chapter Five

While several of us in the Senate were trying to ease the problems in our country, a change occurred. Gradually our university students became militant. They started to demonstrate noisily and in hostile fashion against those same social ills. Their action created a dilemma for me and other senators, especially one named Mekuri—a huge man with a booming voice. "Marta," he said, "I can understand the students' frustrations and complaints, but this isn't the way to go about it."

I agreed. But my worry was for more than just the noise. There seemed to be a dark *spirit* that hovered about the students, which I could discern but not define.

That was altogether too vague, though, to speak about in the Senate, even to Mekuri. When I tried to express it, people's eyebrows would knit. Everyone dismissed my worry except Deme and Father.

"I know," said Deme at dinner one evening, with Father agreeing. "I feel that, too."

Their understanding encouraged me. "It's almost as if the young people are being manipulated," I said. "There are too many strange inconsistencies." We had just gone through an academic strike during which someone threw a bomb into an elementary school classroom! "And lies are tacked onto truth."

With raised fists, the students had recently blamed His Majesty for the famine in the eastern province of Wello. The droughts were real, but to put blame on His Majesty was a horrible distortion of the facts. The truth was that the extent of the famine had been kept secret from the emperor even during one of his visits to the province. When he learned of the cover-up, His Majesty dismissed the governor of the province and ordered immediate relief. He also then appealed for assistance from the world community.

As we talked that evening Deme and I felt we had to *do* something. Father agreed, but reminded us that we had to pray first. "Remember," he said, "prayer without work is dead, but work without prayer is worse."

So we prayed together that night for a way to get to know our students better. As we sought God's direction I thought of Sammy and Mickey now in college in Colorado. Their idealism was admirable and it was hard for me to believe anything else of the students in university here in Ethiopia. Out of our prayers that night came a plan for getting to know student leaders.

The next morning I met with the president of the university student body at a campus coffee shop. I explained that as president of our local YWCA I was in charge of fund-raising. I outlined a plan for a ten-day carnival to celebrate the Y's tenth anniversary, and asked for volunteers. The young man was excited and offered to recruit student helpers.

For the next few weeks Deme and I and our friend Gera spent every spare moment at the carnival site. Thanks to Deme's mechanical skills, pavilions began to mushroom across the field. Gera and I spent time with the students as we planned games and prizes, but I was waiting for a chance to talk with them about their hopes for our country.

That chance soon came. One afternoon as two young men moved a pile of lumber to Gera's restaurant pavilion, a strange thing happened. One of the young men flipped up the point of his shirt collar to show a picture to the other. When I looked questioningly at him he smiled and turned up his collar again so that I could see the picture. It was a portrait of Lenin!

I must have looked startled, because the young man chuckled. "You're like many other Ethiopians. You don't like him, do you, Senator?"

I answered without hesitation. "No, I don't. In my travels

for the government I've seen what happens in Communist countries. But why are you wearing his picture?"

The young man smiled. "It's an identification. Look." He gestured for the other student to turn up the point of his shirt collar. "See? His picture of Mao tells me that he follows the philosophy of the Chinese Communists, and my picture of Lenin tells him who I prefer."

We talked about the different philosophies within Communism, and it became clear that both students were convinced that our country needed to allow "at least a little of the pattern" into our society. At that I shook my head.

"One drop of vinegar spoils a cup of milk."

The young men disagreed. "It won't be that way. We need help. Haile Selassie's government moves much too slowly."

That evening as Gera and Father and Deme and I were discussing the conversations of that afternoon, I felt I still did not have a clear picture of what was happening. "Why don't you call Victor?" Gera suggested. "He's watched all of this before."

It was an excellent idea. Victor was someone who had witnessed at close range the Communists at work in his own Eastern European country. Since he had gone through this already, he would be able to see parallels between our countries.

As soon as I sat down in Victor's office, I told him about the pictures under the students' collars. He ran his hands through his orange hair and stared at the ceiling for a moment before he spoke.

"Yes, I've seen students do the same thing." He paused and frowned as though remembering a pain. "Look, here's what happens. A country has real problems—just as Ethiopia does. People try to bring about reform, but are unsuccessful. The changes don't come. It is right then that the Marxists can organize a power play."

"A power play?"

He nodded. "Yes. Things get worse and worse until finally martial law is declared. Eventually even the military fails. The situation worsens and ultimately results in totalitarianism."

I wanted some hope, but I didn't get it. "Do you think that will happen here?" I asked.

"The Marxists are very clever," Victor said. "They know how to take advantage of some unexpected crisis."

I dreaded to say it. "Such as the famine?"

He nodded his head slowly.

As far as Father was concerned we were living out a prophetic story. He often spoke about what he saw, especially when any of the children were around, as if he were educating them. Mickey, almost 20, was home from college in America for his summer vacation, so he and Bete' and Lali all joined our sober conversations now. Mickey was looking so handsome despite his thinness! I wished his older brother could be with us, too, but Sammy had a summer job in the States.

Mickey and the younger boys and Deme—who was home from the newly purchased coffee and hard beans business in the eastern lowlands city of Dire Dawa—were all seated in the living room at the new house watching television. It was then we learned that the very nature of the crisis His Majesty faced had taken a different, almost mystical turn.

After the Yom Kippur War, the Arabs demanded the withdrawal of Israel from occupied territory and immediately pressed other nations to sever diplomatic relations with Israel. Many African states had begun to do so, and they urged His Majesty to follow. His Majesty was in a difficult position. He took seriously his commitment to the African Unity Charter. In the end he reluctantly severed diplomatic relations with Israel.

Though this action bothered me, too, it was Father's reaction that proved to be prophetic. Father was wrapped in his white *gabby* and looked very much like an ancient patriarch as he nodded or sighed over each item reported on the evening news. Often his wrinkled hands stroked his white beard in concern. Deme and I were only half-listening to the announcer as we talked about Mickey's plans to return to the States.

Suddenly Father spoke in a firm voice. "That's the end of us, you know."

"What?"

He nodded toward the television. "That's the end of our country. We have voted against God's chosen people. Our problems will only worsen now. May God have mercy upon us."

I looked at Deme, half-expecting a tolerant smile.

But Deme's face was as grave as Father's.

We watched problems continue to escalate. First there were mutinies in the armed forces. Then in a series of swift steps the escalation moved into government. The prime minister's cabinet panicked and resigned and was replaced by a new cabinet. But this new cabinet faced demands from both civilian and military groups. The civilians lost ground to the National Security Committee and the Armed Forces Committee, both military groups. Then these two vied for power until the Armed Forces Committee started to arrest men in the National Security Committee, accusing them of being part of the old regime. The Armed Forces Committee began calling itself simply "the Committee." For some reason the very name had an ominous ring.

There were new reports of unrest and fighting within the troops. Teachers went on strike again. Students demonstrated once more, but now without their idealism. One morning on my way into Addis, I found my way blocked by a gathering of young people. To my horror I realized that they were yelling, "Down with the emperor! Kill the emperor!" I was mesmerized by the awful scene as the students raised their fists toward the palace. Tears filled my eyes.

That night at dinner our knowledgeable Eastern European

friend, Victor, joined us. Gera was there, too, waving her tiny hands as she talked. As soon as Father finished asking the blessing, I blurted out the question I had been waiting to ask Victor.

"What do you think of this new group—the Committee?"

Victor tugged at his orange hair as he answered. "Everything you and I talked about is coming to pass. It's time now for the Committee to declare martial law. To stop all of these strikes and demonstrations!"

"Yes," I said. "I've heard the talk already. But how can we allow the Committee to take control?"

Victor had that faraway look again as though he were remembering what had happened in his own country. "So you think the Committee is its own power source?"

I started to answer, but could only stare at him.

"Just what are you trying to say, Victor?" Gera asked. "That someone *else* is behind the power of the Committee?"

He nodded. "Yes. Russia."

"Russia?" Gera said. "What could they possibly want with us?"

Deme answered for Victor. "We are on the Red Sea," he said.

Gera looked bewildered. Victor nodded agreement while Deme continued. "The key is shipping and oil."

Gera wasn't convinced. "If the Russians want our strategic position, why don't they come in with troops?"

Victor shook his head. "The Russians are patient. They know that a country hardly ever falls from outside force. It falls from within. They will wait. Time is on their side."

Suddenly Gera slapped her cheeks with her delicate hands. "That explains it."

"What?"

"You know how men talk when they've been drinking. Well, lately at the restaurant when I bring wine or a bill, I've heard tag ends of conversations about strategy and timing. The talk never made sense until now. I'm going to start listening carefully."

51

Within the next few weeks Victor's scenario took place before our eyes with incredible swiftness. Martial law was declared. Immediately the Committee's "Ethiopia First" slogan appeared everywhere. Action followed the slogans, in the *name* of the slogans. Strikes and demonstrations were not for the good of the country. Public gatherings were banned, "for Ethiopia's sake." There was a midnight-to-dawn curfew in Addis Ababa, "for the well-being of the people." Soldiers loyal to the Committee roamed our streets to enforce the new edicts.

The curfew hampered Deme's coming and going from the business in Dire Dawa, and he didn't get home as often as he would have liked. After a man was shot for being out beyond the allowed time, the rest of us made sure we were home long before the curfew.

One evening, after being in Addis all day, I was anxious to get home before curfew. My thoughts kept centering on His Majesty. Now that he was in his early eighties he looked tired, but he still had an air of independence. Just last week I had seen him with his grandson, Eskinder, who was a rear admiral in the Navy. As they walked, the taller Eskinder bent his head toward his grandfather to continue their conversation. I had wondered if they were discussing the Committee.

Suddenly, a few hundred meters from our driveway, across the road, I came to a military barrier.

It had been constructed while I was away. A little house sat in floodlights on the right side of the road. A long wooden pole stretched across the pavement blocking traffic in both directions. Next to each pole stood a soldier with a rifle at the ready. A lieutenant came out of the posthouse, his hand resting on the gun in his shoulder holster. He asked for my identification.

I fumbled for my driver's license and handed it to him, angry with myself for being nervous. Finally the young man thrust my license back at me. "Where are you going?"

I pointed to our home. "I live in the green house."

He nodded and waved for the soldier to swing up the gate pole. I wanted to hurry away but forced myself to smile as I drove slowly past the soldiers and turned toward the safety of home.

Morning radio broadcasts began to take on new importance now since daily instructions—such as changes in the curfew hour and off-limit areas—were given. We all listened carefully. Father and Mickey (who had not yet returned to the States) joined Bete', Lali and me in the dining room. It should have been a warm family time as we shared the traditional Ethiopian breakfast of butter poured over cracked wheat. But the joy was gone. Each morning the emotionless voice on the radio brought news of some new step the Committee had taken.

One weekend morning we were settled into our usual places. Deme was with us and Assafa was wordlessly offering him more fruit when the room was suddenly filled with an eerie military march blaring from the radio.

We all darted looks at one another. Little Lali clutched his grandfather's arm. As the sinister blend of drums and cymbals continued, goose bumps crawled toward my scalp. I closed my hand around Deme's arm. Bete' frowned toward Mickey. Assafa was rooted to the floor, gripping the tray of fruit. Strong male voices began to sing words to the horrible rhythm: "Let's stand for Ethiopia. Let no blood be shed." As their voices faded away, they were replaced with the sweet sounds of children singing to the same martial tune.

The music stopped and the cold voice of the announcer stated, among other things, that all student passports had been canceled.

Mickey blanched. Deme and I could only stare at one another. The announcer droned on. Ethiopia provided education for its youth, he said, so it was unnecessary to look elsewhere.

At Deme's motion, Assafa snapped off the radio.

53

One day while I was visiting Gera the doorbell rang. When Gera answered it, there stood Mekuri, the big man who had worked for reform with me in the Senate. Mekuri was tense. "Marta! You're here! I tried calling you. They've arrested seven cabinet members!"

I covered my ears with my hands, then let them fall uselessly to my side as I had a terrifying thought. "Mekuri, is His Majesty all right?"

Mekuri frowned at me. "His Majesty? Of course. I just saw him. Surely you don't think they would arrest him?"

Then he was out the door, as though looking for someone else to tell his news to. I shut my eyes wondering who had been arrested.

What would happen now? The Committee was at our very throat.

We turned on the radio after dinner. The awful march started again. The announcer's voice read off a list of cabinet members who had been arrested, then added the names of the rest of the cabinet, not yet in custody. Each had 24 hours to turn himself in or all his property would be confiscated. The march sounded its eerie, threatening tones.

The arrests didn't stop. All the next week additional names were added to the list.

Then came the horrible news that Eskinder, His Majesty's grandson, had been arrested. I cried as I remembered how recently I had seen them walking together. The word was that the Committee was holding its prisoners in storage rooms in the basement of the palace.

Long before Mekuri told me of the cabinet members' arrests, I had considered resigning from the Senate. Now I could no longer postpone that dreaded decision.

It was a beautiful June morning in 1974 and Deme was home for a few days from Dire Dawa. I blurted out my decision.

"Deme, I'm going to resign. I refuse to cooperate with these men."

Deme nodded. "Yes," he said, "I knew this would come. But what will you say in your letter? It isn't wise to be blunt."

I bit my lip. I wanted the Committee to know how I felt, yet calling them madmen would serve no purpose right now.

I sat at my desk, blank paper before me. Finally I took the cap off my pen and began a letter of resignation from government service, the very thing I had worked for all my life. I simply stated that it was no longer possible for me to serve my country as I wished.

I wanted so much to see His Majesty. His role in all that was happening truly puzzled me. His Majesty was a paternalistic and benevolent man. Was he so accustomed to the power that comes with centuries of continuous rule, however, that he was perhaps naive? Had he been so generous that it was difficult for him to imagine people being disloyal? After all, the various military groups had repeatedly pledged their loyalty to him.

The only way I could question His Majesty's silence was to think that perhaps people around him prevented him from knowing what was going on. Someone had to confront him. Someone had to urge him to flee, to set up a government in exile. It seemed odd that I should be the one to try.

It was then that I asked for and was granted the private meeting with him in his office.

When I returned home that rainy July morning, I went right to bed, sick with disappointment at His Majesty's refusal to listen to my warning. He had said I was a worrisome woman. Indeed! Now I was convinced there was no turning back from the course of destruction our country had taken.

A week later Deme and I were invited to a midday meal (the nighttime curfew was still in effect) with one of Deme's business associates. Another guest was gold-toothed Zelke, the man who years ago suggested that I not take the Senate so seriously.

After dinner Zelke asked me to join him on the veranda. We sat on one of the little stone benches, and Zelke leaned uncomfortably close to me.

"Marta, you disappoint me. Why haven't you been on the radio?"

"On the radio? Do you think it would help? I'll gladly do whatever I can."

He leaned still closer, his narrow eyes a contrast to his wide mouth filled with all those gold teeth. "Yes, they'd be happy to have you help with their efforts to bring in a new system."

A new system? "Zelke, you want me to speak in favor of the Committee?"

He chuckled. "Well, of course! The old ways are gone, Marta."

It was useless to talk further. I made one final comment before going to find Deme. "No, Zelke, I won't help them destroy my country."

The next morning the phone rang during breakfast. The caller's voice was muffled.

"Marta? You must leave. Your name just came on the list."

"What list? Who is this?"

"I can't explain, but you are going to be arrested."

The phone went dead. I sat staring at the receiver as Deme came in.

"Marta, what's wrong?"

I tried to make light of the call, saying that someone was playing a trick. Deme wasn't fooled.

"No, Marta, that was not a trick. Addis isn't safe for you anymore. Come down to Dire Dawa with me—all of you. The Committee isn't too powerful yet in the provinces. We'll stay there until things calm down."

"And what if things never do calm down? What about the business?"

Deme sat on the sofa next to me. "We have much to decide, Marta," he said. "I want to keep the business open as long as I can. The chances are that we will lose everything. Meanwhile, over a thousand people in Dire Dawa depend on us to keep our doors open. As long as we can."

I looked at the deep lines in his face, lines that hadn't been there before. "Deme," I said, "what do you mean, lose everything?" I thought of the years, the sacrifices that had gone into building all that we had.

"You know the Marxist history as well as I do," he replied. "We'll be lucky to save our lives."

I nodded, thinking of all the people who had been shot for breaking some insignificant rule. "Who knows?" I said. "They may someday start shooting the students."

Deme stood up and gestured toward the roses beyond the veranda. "Even something as lovely as our home isn't important. People, and our integrity—that's what's important."

I squeezed my eyes shut, trying not to be overcome by tears. "Oh, Deme, I'm so glad Sammy's safe in the States."

I knew that underneath it all, Deme was saying we would have to leave, not just Addis Ababa, but our beloved country.

That afternoon we began to make our plans to go to Dire Dawa. I had taken it for granted that Father would come with us. But he shook his head.

"No. I'm not leaving Addis. I can pray for my country better here in my own home than I can down there in Dire Dawa."

I didn't give up easily, and I begged him to come with us. Still he refused.

Well, if he wouldn't go to Dire Dawa, at least we would make sure he was well taken care of. Only Assafa would accompany us to the lowlands; the rest of the staff would stay on to care for Father. That also gave the appearance that our trip to Dire Dawa was just a short visit. As soon as I said that to myself, I realized I was already learning the importance of secrecy. Outside of the household, only Gera and my old Senate reform friend Mekuri knew we were going to Dire Dawa.

One morning just before we were to leave, Mekuri arrived at our home. In his big booming voice he announced that he had a going-away present for me. Then he unwrapped the oddly shaped package he had brought with him. It was a submachine gun!

"Why are you giving me this?" I managed to stammer.

Never before that moment had I heard him whisper. But now he did. "These aren't peaceful times. I'll feel better if you have a gun."

"But an automatic weapon?"

He shrugged. "You may not have time to reload."

For the next hour he insisted on showing me how to load the gun, how to hold it, and how to clean and oil it. He wanted to take me into the mountains to practice firing it, but I refused.

After Mekuri left, I wrestled with a heavy problem. How far would I go in self-protection? As a Christian should I use a gun? Shouldn't I be trusting more in God's protection and less in my own?

But as I struggled, I imagined soldiers pointing rifles at the faces of my sons. The image was so real that I suddenly knew I would do whatever I had to in order to protect them.

As we were about to leave, events took a new turn. Victor had said that the Marxists take advantage of a crisis, and once again he was right. The Committee had long been blaming the famine on His Majesty, but now they began a full-scale media accusation. Famine conditions in Wello were shown on television and in posters. Next to the pictures were contrasting photographs of His Majesty at a palace dinner.

Their intent to malign him was obvious and I couldn't deny

that both scenes were true. We *did* have a terrible famine within our borders, and His Majesty *had* hosted expensive state dinners. But the famine hadn't come because of imperial greed as the Committee was trying to say. His Majesty wasn't a selfish ruler and he wasn't guilty of the sin of an uncaring heart.

The military march continued to be played daily. Each time we heard it we would freeze, knowing that another list of arrests was about to be read. The lists no longer contained just the names of those in political office; they also included those who had received gifts of cars and homes from His Majesty. I held my breath, listening for my name. Hadn't His Majesty provided our first home in honor of the service Mickey's and Sammy's father had given to Ethiopia?

But my name wasn't read. As I pondered that unbelievable oversight on the part of the Committee, I remembered that the promised title to that house had never been sent to us. And the house was ultimately turned back to His Majesty's estate. Years ago I had been hurt by the oversight, but now I was thankful for the error and saw it as God's sheltering.

And while I was still thinking about the undelivered title, a list was read of those who had received government scholarships for their children to study abroad. Mekuri's name was on that list!

My sons, too, had studied abroad. But we had paid all their bills because the promised scholarships had been overlooked by the Ministry of Education. Now I wondered if there was a pattern to all of this. Had the Lord been protecting our family back then from this future danger? But why? We certainly weren't special. And if He had chosen to protect us, why had He done so? What did He have for us to do?

On the morning we were to leave for Dire Dawa, Gera came to say goodbye. I saw her car pull into our drive, and I ran across our veranda and down the wide steps to greet her. She stopped the car next to the crimson rosebushes and gestured wildly for me to get in.

As soon as I closed the door, her tiny hands gripped my arm. "Marta! I've just heard that you were almost arrested!"

So the telephone warning had been real! "How did you hear that?"

"Never mind—people talk in restaurants, remember? I'm telling you that you would have been arrested if the Committee wasn't having problems of its own right now. When you get to Dire Dawa, stay out of sight. Give the Committee a chance to forget you."

"For how long, Gera?"

"Who knows—six months? Just stay out of sight."

So we left for Dire Dawa that afternoon, in July 1974, planning not to slip back to Addis for a long time.

Chapter Six

Gera kept in touch. She told us she'd heard nothing more about our arrest, but urged us still to keep a low profile. So it wasn't until the night of September 11, 1974, that Deme and I risked an after-dark-but-before-curfew drive back into Addis Ababa to spend a few hours with Father. It had been two months since we'd seen him. Just as we were entering the city we passed a convoy of army vehicles. I could sense Deme's anxiety as he nodded toward the trucks.

"Look," he said, "something must be wrong."

"What could it be?"

"I wish I knew. Every one of the trucks is filled with combat-ready troops."

"Oh, Deme, do be careful."

We drove the rest of the way without speaking again. At the military barrier near our house the guard looked at our I.D.'s and back at us twice. We held our breath, hoping that Gera had been right about the orders for our arrest being side-tracked. Finally, with one more careful look at us, the guard waved us through.

Just before the 7:00 a.m. news the next morning Deme and Father and I were in the living room. I stood in front of the open window, looking at my beautiful mountains.

"Marta, it's time for the news," Deme said. "Come."

I sat on the sofa next to Deme. Father was in his favorite chair by the window. The broadcast started. As the dreaded march sounded, I gripped Deme's hand and we waited through those drums and cymbals, through the frenzied singing of the soldiers and the ironic sweetness of the children's voices.

At last the flat voice of the announcer came on. "This morning Emperor Haile Selassie I resigned. He has been replaced by a military leadership that will at last seek the good of all Ethiopia."

We looked at one another in horror. The voice continued.

"Parliament is abolished and a new constitution will go into effect as soon as order is established."

The rest of the broadcast was lost in the clamor of our questions. It took hours for us to find out what had really happened. Early that morning, it was said, His Majesty had been called into the library of the palace, where Committee officers read a proclamation accusing him of corruption and neglect and of using the throne for personal gain. He was, the Committee said, too old and weak to continue his rule. His Majesty reportedly answered that he had served his people in war and peace. "But," he added, "if we have to step down for the good of our people, we will not oppose this."

Deme and I knew that we had to go back to Dire Dawa immediately. We asked Father again to come with us, but he shook his head. "I shall remain here until the Lord calls me to be with Him. I shall pray for my country."

With tears running down my cheeks, I hugged him good-bye.

I summarized all of these events in a letter to Sammy. I doubted the letter would get through by regular post since the mails were almost certainly being censored, so I gave it to a visitor who was flying to the States, asking him to post the letter to Sammy from New York. I told Sammy about the arrest of members of the royal family, down to the grand-children.

I told him that His Majesty had been confined to one small room at the palace. I told him how a "friend of ours who owns a restaurant" heard soldiers joking about His Majesty. He was still the Lion of Judah, the soldiers said, but now he was a pathetic *caged* lion.

I sent the letter to Sammy—even with all of the tear stains.

In November 1974, two months after His Majesty's arrest, Deme and I returned to Addis Ababa again, this time to offer condolences to the families of 62 men who had just been massacred by the Committee.

I had learned of the executions down in Dire Dawa. I had been driving in my car, and had just turned on the radio. That awful march was playing, and I gripped the steering wheel, knowing that the news to follow wouldn't be good. When the last of the singing voices faded, the monotone voice said, "Sixty-two of Ethiopia's enemies have been executed." I gasped with the first name, pulled over to the side of the road, and began to sob as each new name was read. I knew them all! The list included the prime minister, cabinet members, heads of departments, military officials, even senators.

Then the emotionless voice read the name of His Majesty's grandson Eskinder. No! Why had they killed him? Why had they killed any of them?

And in wide-eyed terror I heard the name of my dear friend Mekuri! Was that booming voice really silenced forever? My sobs drowned out the rest of the names.

By the time I arrived home my tears were a mixture of sorrow and fury. How could this thing have happened in a civilized country? There had been no trial, even though the men had been promised one. How could the Committee just take 62 men out of prison and shoot them?

Still crying, I ran into the house and grabbed my recorder so I could tape the list when it was announced again. I wanted to have proof of this terrible thing so that it wouldn't be forgotten. As I thrust the plug of the recorder into the wall, I determined that someday I would let the world know what had happened. These men couldn't remain faceless statistics!

Now here we were back in Addis and doing something I knew was very dangerous. Deme and I were going to visit the families of the murdered men, even though the Committee encouraged people to turn in anyone who spoke against the new government. There were spies throughout the city, and what better place to add to their list than at the homes of the families of each man who had been killed? But dangerous or not, we had to be here.

We drove to Mekuri's home first. There were several cars parked in front of the gray stucco dwelling, so I knew the house was filled with those who had come to grieve with Mekuri's widow and son. We hurried to join them, but just as we started to enter through the gate of the stone fence, we heard a gasp behind us.

"Marta! How foolish you are!"

Startled, we turned to see Mekuri's secretary. She grabbed both of our arms and almost pushed us into the house as she spoke again. "You shouldn't be seen on the streets. Do you want this terrible thing to happen to you, too?"

I shook my head. "We had to come. We couldn't stay away. Please excuse us. We must see his family."

Inside the house, Mekuri's widow and son were seated. A picture of Mekuri in his senatorial cloak was on the small table near them. There were many people in the room, some talking quietly, others crying. Mekuri's family greeted us and we hugged one another as we cried together. His widow kept whispering between sobs, "To think that you actually came here. . . ." We knew we had done the right thing.

While we were there, we began to get a picture of what had happened to the 62 men.

Over 300 important figures had been imprisoned in the palace basement, in addition to hundreds of others held in regular prisons. We were told that on the night of the massacre, soldiers went to the palace to pick up the men who were to be shot. On the way to the execution grounds they stopped at a hospital to demand the release of a general who was there. The nurse refused to unhook the I.V. from the general's arm, but a guard jerked it out so the soldiers could take him with them. When other prisoners in the truck saw the general being dragged out of the hospital, they tried to protest. One prisoner told a soldier he wasn't a real man to treat his own countrymen that way. The soldier hit him in the face with his rifle butt.

People living near the main prison said the truck stopped inside the walls. They had watched in terror from nearby darkened windows earlier that day as a large trench had been dug. Now, one by one, the 62 men were shot and their bodies pushed into the hole. A shovelful of lime was tossed on top of each body.

We left Mekuri's home and went to the next on our tragic list and continued to hear the same horrible stories. At each home we visited during the next four days we tried to comfort the families as they wondered what those last few minutes had been like for their husbands, brothers, fathers, sons. I could offer no reassuring words. I could offer only myself by being there.

Everywhere we visited, we also heard about the one man on the Committee who had tried to prevent the murder of the 62. Among other demands of the Committee, General Aman was supposed to sign the death sentences of those men massacred. He refused. Representatives from the Committee went to his home to talk with him, but he would not see them. They fired their guns at his home. He returned fire. Soon a tank was positioned in front of the house and began to fire heavy artillery through the walls! When General Aman still didn't come out, the tank crashed through the walls of the house. Members of the Committee found the general's body in the bedroom; he had committed suicide rather than be taken.

Deme and I drove to General Aman's house. The reports had not been exaggerated. We saw the white plaster walls leaning against one another, the remains of the floor covered with broken cement blocks and splintered furniture.

Back in Dire Dawa we heard reports every day of some new atrocity. Over the weeks the details became more horrifying. People who resisted arrest were shot instantly, their riddled bodies left where they fell. After four months of this kind of terror, freedom fighters sprang up to resist the Committee. When they were caught they were executed.

Then came the turning point for us. One more group of freedom fighters was captured. The men were beheaded, and their bloody bodies shown on television as a warning.

That did it. Deme looked at me and spoke for the first time the thought I had been suppressing for a long time.

"We'll have to escape, Marta," he said.

It was out. Deme tried to make his words sound even and casual, but it didn't work. They were charged. Leave our own country? Leave the land we both loved?

"When we were in college we promised to serve. . . ." I couldn't finish my sentence.

Never had I heard Deme sigh so sorrowfully. "Let's admit what we've known for a long time, Marta. We *have* to leave. Perhaps we can serve Ethiopia best now by running away from her."

The awful moment had finally come. I held back my tears as, that very night, we began to make quiet inquiries. Yes, people were trying to flee. Some made it out. Some were caught and shot. The best route was south to Kenya.

Our plans were thwarted before they began because our special, quiet, wonderful Mickey became ill.

For days I had noticed that Mickey was constantly tired. He wasn't eating well, either. At first I did typical motherly things like pile his plate high and insist that he rest. His skin turned yellow-orange and he began to vomit. The diagnosis was hepatitis. After a month in the Dire Dawa hospital, Mickey was no better and his doctors agreed that he must return to Addis for a blood transfusion.

Deme had known for weeks he would have to abandon the business, but he wanted to stay in Dire Dawa long enough to see that the last payroll was properly prepared. The boys and I flew home. As soon as we arrived I put Mickey to bed; and while Assafa brought in glasses of water and orange juice, which Mickey needed for the jaundice, I called the hospital. To my intense disappointment, there were no rooms available, but would I try again in two days? Meanwhile, have the young man rest and give him plenty of water and juices.

"Lord, You know that the doctors have said the blood transfusion is needed. Mickey could die. Oh, please allow him to get into the hospital now."

I wanted the room to be filled with sunshine as a sign that my prayer would be answered. But there was no sudden brilliance and no miraculous ringing of the phone with a message saying a room was ready after all.

"All right, Lord," I whispered. "Help me walk by faith and not by sight. I give Mickey's future—and ours—to You." Then I remembered Deme's prayer and added, "We will do what we can and leave the results to You."

I turned away from the phone, anxious to be with Mickey, little realizing how we were going to need that prayer.

That afternoon many of our friends came to visit. They were alarmed that we had come back. Gera, especially, waved her tiny hands in horror and shook her head over our risk-taking. But she did have news of His Majesty which she had gleaned, as always, from her quiet eavesdropping at the restaurant. She told us that a guard was always with His Majesty, under orders not to speak to him except on business and never to use the imperial title. One day His Majesty asked the guard how long he had been in the army. Startled, the guard forgot not only his orders but also his instructions about forms of address.

"Eleven years, Your Majesty."

His Majesty looked toward the guard, seeming to stare at a point beyond his head. "Then we brought you up. We educated you. And now you are a traitor to your country."

The soldier, Gera said, had tears in his eyes as he told the story to his friend in her restaurant.

Our second day back in Addis was August 27, 1975. Lali and Bete' were squeezing orange juice for Mickey while Father (dressed as always in his white *gabby*) and I had lunch together. Over coffee, the two of us talked while the radio played softly in the background.

Suddenly the threatening march of the Committee came on the air. We froze, knowing that the Committee was about to announce some new horrible deed.

The music stopped. There was a pause. I could hear the ticking of the clock from the next room.

The announcer said, "Here is a late bulletin. The previous emperor, who had been ill, was found dead in his quarters last night, and his funeral has taken place."

With that terse statement the music began again. The children's voices sang, "Let's stand for Ethiopia. Let no blood be shed . . . ."

I sat stunned. But not Father. He was on his feet.

"Marta, please excuse me. I must fast and pray for my country."

I started to get up, but he gestured for me to remain seated. His words were strained. "No, this is my work now. You must do what you must do. My prayers are for us all."

I watched him turn to leave, his head down. What did he mean about my doing what I must? Had he guessed that Deme and I were planning to leave Ethiopia as soon as we could? Was he telling me goodbye? I knew he would never go with us. He wouldn't even go to Dire Dawa! I wanted to run after him, cling to him, and kiss him goodbye. With tears running down my cheeks, I whispered what I somehow sensed even then might be a farewell to my father.

I couldn't wait for Deme to finish closing down his affairs. We needed him here now! I went to tell the boys about His Majesty's death. The two young ones, Lali (10) and Bete' (15), understood little of the full significance of his death, but Mickey's eyes told me that he, at 22, grasped all too well that the last major symbol of an era had now perished.

Gera came to the house to find me wearing a black skirt and sweater—a poor substitute for the screams welling up inside me.

"Gera," I said, "I want to show the world that I am in mourning. I'm going out."

"You can't, Marta! That's just asking for trouble."

"I *will* go, my dear. And now. They can't tell me not to mourn."

Brave little Gera came with me. We headed out the gate, managing to appear calm as we passed through the checkpoint at the top of the hill. "Let's go to the palace," I said. Gera shrugged helplessly. I expected to find groups of people gathered on the corners, ignoring the Committee and mourning the emperor's death. But the streets were empty. Had the Committee so successfully destroyed three thousand years of history that the people didn't care to mourn?

When we arrived at the palace, the gates were shut and locked, unguarded except by the silent stone lions on top of their pillars. The Committee wasn't even going to allow mourning; they were going to pretend that His Majesty had never existed.

What I wanted to do was get out of the car and stand defiantly in my black mourning clothes before the gate. But reason prevailed. Like those great doors, my beloved Ethiopia was shut and locked.

Chapter Seven

Deme arrived the day after His Majesty's death. As soon as he opened the door, we clung to each other and cried.

We went to Mickey's room. Even though it had been just a few days since Deme had seen Mickey, I could tell by his solemn voice that he wasn't prepared for the deterioration that had taken place. Mickey, naturally slender, was now just plain frail. His skin, which should have been honey toned, was now a sickly orange. Deme sat on the edge of the bed and took Mickey's hand into his own as he spoke.

"Son, we're trying to get you into the hospital. Is there anything I can do for you?"

Mickey gripped Deme's hand. "No, Dad. I'm just tired. What's going to happen to the business now?"

Deme started to speak, but apparently he couldn't trust his voice. He patted Mickey on the shoulder and motioned for me to leave with him. As we walked back to the living room, Deme rubbed his hand across his forehead and whispered: "Marta, we don't have as much time as I thought. We must leave fast. Tomorrow."

"Tomorrow!" Startled, I closed the door to the dining room.

Deme began to pace nervously. When finally he spoke, his voice was tense. "We're on the list to be arrested with the next group—along with Zelke."

Zelke? That gold-toothed charlatan was on *their* side?

"What about Mickey?"

A terrible sadness swept over Deme's face. "Yes, I know. If we leave him behind, he can get his transfusions, but the Committee would punish him for our escape. If we take him with us, he may die before we can get him to the hospital in Kenya."

70

Now it was my turn to pace. If only we had another month to make plans. If only we could have gotten Mickey into the Addis hospital immediately. If only we knew someone who could get us safely through the Kenyan desert. If only. . . .

Suddenly I was too tired to question any longer. I sat down on the sofa. Deme knelt next to me, took my hands, and began to pray that God would give us strength for the time ahead of us. He prayed for wisdom about Mickey. At his whispered "Amen," I put my hand on his shoulder. "Deme, I can't leave him here. I want him with us."

He nodded. "I agree. We'll just have to trust the Lord for his safety as well as ours. But we must tell him nothing. And we must pray that the Lord will seal the boys' lips so that they won't ask questions. No one must know—except your father, so he can pack."

Tears began to run down my cheeks. "Oh, Deme, Father won't go. You know he won't. He's in seclusion. He won't even talk to me."

Deme's sigh seemed to come from his very heart. "You're right. Then we must be careful not to tell him. His life depends on his not knowing a thing about our plans."

We were silent. From the kitchen at the back of the house I could hear dishes being taken out of the cabinets. Soon Assafa would call us to lunch and would take a tray up to Mickey while Deme and I chatted with Lali and Bete' and pretended that everything was normal.

Deme stood looking out through the French doors past the veranda and beyond the stone fence toward the mountains. He was taking deep breaths as though implanting the spicy smell of eucalyptus into his memory. I stood next to him, my arm through his. There were the rosebushes with their array of color . . . and the majestic fig tree . . . the distant mountains . . . all part of a scene that we would never see again. We were saying goodbye to the house we had built together.

And what was the sum of those years? My work in the Senate had never yielded the fruit of reform. Some unknown person would take over the business in Dire Dawa. None of this made sense now. We didn't even have time to plan carefully for our escape.

"Please, Lord. I can do nothing. You alone can take us through. Help me to be alert to Your provision. Help me to listen and to obey, knowing that Your directions will never contradict the Scriptures. We are helpless. You are our strength."

We experienced four frightening, frustrating days as we dealt with a man whose code name was "Wolde." To rent his Land Rover cost two-and-a-half times the price of a new vehicle, but we could not buy a Land Rover without calling attention to our escape plans. At least the price included a driver and guide. "Wolde says we'll need the help," Deme reported. "We'll have to leave the main road and travel through dry riverbeds."

Finally the day came when I asked our cook to prepare a Sunday picnic for the family. Cook fixed a gala lunch of chicken breasts, a loaf of fresh bread, a small jar of marmalade, oranges, tangerines, fruit juices, and a one day's supply of water.

As I watched her prepare the food, I suddenly wanted to include something from my home that would remind us of the happy times we had enjoyed here. It would have to be appropriate for a luncheon basket. I walked into the formal dining room and looked around at all the lovely things.

Ah, the glasses! I opened the china cabinet and selected a set of four pink crystal glasses that a visiting president had given me after a state visit. There were five of us, plus the guide and driver, but never mind! I took the glasses carefully into my hands, and then looked around the room. How often we had entertained friends here. Twenty-four smiling faces around the table, enjoying our hospitality, none of us dreaming that we would be caught in a nightmare.

So many memories were in that room. On the tea cart was

the sterling silver tea service His Majesty and Her Majesty had given us as a wedding present. And there were the silver cups they had given each of my sons. Even now I could hear the sound of their teeth clinking against the rims—but I couldn't take those in a luncheon basket! Resolutely I turned and walked back to the kitchen, holding only the glasses. I handed them to the cook. "Please add these to the basket."

The cook looked surprised. "These? But they are your good ones."

I tried to sound casual. "Yes, but we're going out toward Lake Langano and I'd like this lunch to be special." Lake Langano was a favorite resort area for government officials. "Please pack them."

The cook shrugged her shoulders, wrapped the glasses in paper towels, and tucked them into the corners of the basket. I turned to go. Then, hoping I still sounded casual, I turned back to her.

"Oh, we won't be back until Wednesday. Why don't you go see your mother? Assafa will look after Father when he breaks his fast."

She smiled her agreement. At last everything was going well. By Wednesday we would already have been in Kenya for a day.

I'm glad that I didn't know then just how wrong I was.

I went into Mickey's bedroom. Deme, Lali, and Bete' were there, organizing a checkers tournament. I fluffed Mickey's pillow and eased it back under his head. If only he wasn't that awful orange color. . . .

As though he had seen the worry in my eyes, Mickey spoke. "Mom, I'm feeling some better, but—" He looked over at his youngest brother and winked. "But don't tell Lali or he won't let me win at checkers."

"Marta, have you packed for us?" Deme interrupted.

"I'll do that right now."

Mickey's eyes caught mine as I turned to go. They were

steady, but the fun that was in his voice as he had joked with Lali and Bete' was nowhere in his eyes. Did Mickey know? After all, he was a young man now. He was perfectly aware of the danger I faced as a former senator and childhood protegee of the throne. Was I reading in those quiet eyes that our Mickey knew and was playing the game for the sake of the younger boys?

I opened the suitcase on our bed. Wolde had said we could take only two valises for the five of us, so I had to choose carefully. An extra suit for Deme, two dresses for me, under-clothes, sweaters. I folded them carefully and closed the lid. Suddenly my helplessness overpowered me and I cried, whispering, "Please be with us, Lord."

I went into the bathroom to wash my face. This, I reminded myself again, was just a short vacation trip. What if one of the household help found me crying? For their safety as well as our own, I must pretend that everything was normal.

Deme came in. "The Land Rover is here. The driver will want the luggage."

I gestured toward the closed suitcase on our bed, glad that because of Deme's business it was not unusual for strange men to arrive at the house driving dusty, rugged vehicles. Through the window I could see three men get out of the Land Rover and approach the steps. One of them must be Wolde. Deme squeezed my hand as the doorbell rang. We went down.

Deme opened the front door, and suddenly I was hesitant. Should we have made arrangements to meet these men somewhere else? How trustworthy was Wolde? He had already missed all of the appointments we had set up. What if his men thought we were carrying a great deal of money instead of the little we had? What if Wolde demanded a higher price? What if. . . .

Please, Lord, help me to remember that I've already given the future to You.

Deme turned to me. "Marta, this is Wolde."

74

I smiled and then invited Wolde and his men into the living room. For a few moments no one spoke as we all tried to look each other over without appearing to do just that.

Wolde was short and heavy, with a receding hairline. His shirt was clean but it was a size too small and pulled open across his stomach. Wolde spoke first, gesturing toward the fine-boned man who was searching his pockets for something: "This is Rebe, your driver."

Rebe pulled out a package of cigarettes. Now he began to look for an ashtray, but somehow his glances seemed furtive, as if he spent a great deal of time looking over his shoulder. I handed him the ashtray we kept for guests. How old was he? Thirty, perhaps?

Wolde spoke again. "And this is Lemma, your guide. He's from the border area where you must cross and knows the trails well."

We turned to greet the tall young man who sat quietly in the armchair. When he smiled at us, I saw how much whiter his teeth were than Rebe's tobacco-stained teeth. Lemma was also slim and had delicate bone structure, which accented his thin, long nose. I hoped he was stronger than he looked.

Assafa brought in cakes and coffee on a tray and passed them to our guests. After Assafa left, Wolde sipped the coffee, but he often glanced at the door to the dining room, which our steward had left open when he returned to the kitchen. Deme stood up to close the door. Wolde spoke.

"Your luggage is ready? Good. We'll take it now. One more thing—where are your guns?"

Guns? My mind reeled. Were those words actually being spoken in our living room and not in some spy movie? Deme was already heading for our bedroom to get the gun Mekuri had given me.

Deme returned immediately and placed a canvas bag near our suitcases. "We are prepared," he said solemnly.

Wolde nodded and stood up. "Rebe will show you the route."

Rebe pulled a piece of paper from his shirt pocket and spread it out on the coffee table. The rest of us clustered around. There before us was the picture of our escape!

Rebe, still gripping his cigarette butt, pointed to the X in the center of the map.

"O.K., here's Addis. The drive over the new highway into Kenya *should* take just eleven hours. But we'll need a lot longer. We can't go by the new road much of the way; it's too heavily guarded."

Deme and I knew that highway well. It was a two-lane blacktop that in peacetime could have taken us directly into Kenya.

Rebe tapped the map again. "O.K., we start out in Addis and end up here in Marsabit, Kenya. That's your sanctuary."

I interrupted. "But we want to get to Nairobi."

Rebe shrugged. "Marsabit is the first town beyond the desert. You can rent a car there. We'll get you through the desert and that's it."

He tapped the map again. "O.K., between Addis and Marsabit we have four danger spots—the towns of Arbaminch, Yabello, and Mega, and then of course the desert."

He pointed to the map as he continued: "Arbaminch is the first danger spot because there are a lot of students there who'd just love to turn you over to the Committee. We can't go *around* Arbaminch because of the ditches and mucky fields. So we'll time it and go through town during the rush hour. We can hope nobody will pay any attention to us."

The ash from his cigarette dropped onto the already dirty map, and I wondered how many people before us he had explained the route to. He blew the ash away and then pointed to the next X just beyond Arbaminch.

"Here is Yabelo. That's bad because of the treacherous road crew. They've actually turned people over to the soldiers, so we don't want to get stopped here."

Next he pointed to the X at the town of Mega, near the border. "This is the most dangerous town of all because they've doubled the police at the outpost. This place bristles with fences and ditches. We won't go through Mega—we'll try to make it across the sand dunes."

Deme looked up from the map. "Is this Land Rover sturdy enough for the riverbeds and sand?"

Wolde spoke angrily. "Of course it is! If you don't want to trust me, there are plenty of people who need my help."

Rebe interrupted. "The vehicle is O.K. Look." He tapped the map again. "We'll cross the border at this point. That doesn't mean we're safe. Soldiers have followed people right into Kenya and arrested them there. But the main thing we've got to worry about is that desert."

He pointed to the innocent-looking area between Mega and Marsabit as he continued. "If all goes well we'll cross most of the desert before dawn. We'd better! During the day the temperature gets up to 120 degrees."

Why was I suddenly worried? Wolde's voice cut through my thoughts before they had fully formed.

"You'll leave at 8:00 sharp, tonight." Deme and I looked at each other. So long?! "You are to drive to our rendezvous outside town in your own car. We'll be waiting with the Land Rover. I'll bring your car back. Don't be late."

I wanted to tell *him* not to be late, after all his delays. But I kept silent as he and Deme shook hands.

Wolde and his men picked up our luggage and the gun bag and walked out to their Land Rover. Deme and I followed them out. As they stowed the gun bag and hid it with the suitcases I studied the vehicle. Most Land Rovers around Addis were made entirely of metal, but this one was the type used in the hot lowlands around Dire Dawa. It looked like a white pickup truck with a dirty canvas top framing the cargo area. Through the windshield I could see the cab area with its little window between the driver's seat and the back compartment.

Rebe gestured toward the back where the suitcases were. "Lemma will sit back there with your sons. You and your husband will be in the front with me."

I did not nod. My eyes were on the rear compartment. Most

Land Rovers have bench cushions back there, but this one had nothing but the gritty seat. How was Mickey going to fare?

Wolde closed the door and mumbled, "Tonight," as his farewell. Deme and I watched the three men drive away, and held our breath as the Land Rover moved safely through the military checkpoint outside our compound. We went back inside to wait through the last few hours in our home. I had to tell the cook we'd be late getting off, and that the food should be kept cool.

When I returned to the living room the phone was ringing. Deme grabbed the receiver. "Yes?" His face turned ashen. He looked at me, his eyes troubled. "Yes, I understand. Thank you." He put down the phone.

"Deme, what's wrong?"

"That was Gera. They've arrested Zelke."

Zelke arrested? The memory of his gold teeth flashed before me. Our names were on the same list. His arrest meant that our time was short.

Deme and I prayed. "Lord, help us to get out. But if that isn't Your will, help us to face with courage whatever is ahead."

We sat quietly, holding hands. I thought of my father, still praying in his bedroom and still refusing to see anyone. He had been in that little room fasting since the death of His Majesty four days ago. He said he would pray for all of us. Suddenly I knew that Father was making this escape with us, in his own way.

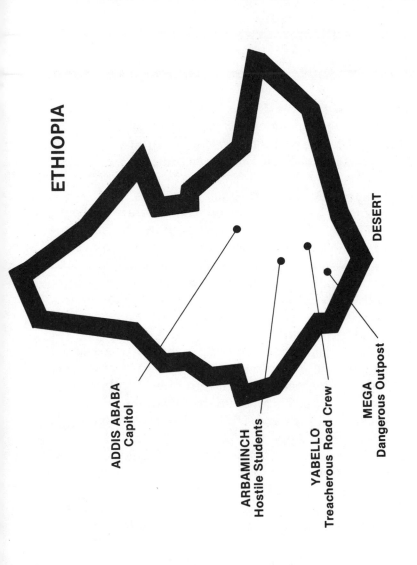

ETHIOPIA

ADDIS ABABA
Capitol

ARBAMINCH
Hostile Students

YABELLO
Treacherous Road Crew

MEGA
Dangerous Outpost

DESERT

MARSABIT
Sanctuary

Chapter Eight

Sunday, August 31, 1975. 8:00 p.m. At the palace headquarters of the Committee.

Although we didn't know it at the time, at this hour a young lieutenant was being handed a piece of paper by his superior officer. On it were two names—mine and Deme's. The lieutenant was ordered to arrest us both at dawn the next morning.

Sunday, August 31. 8:00 p.m. At our home.

The last moment had finally arrived. It was torture not being able to kiss Father farewell. We said goodbye to the staff, casually—all except Assafa, who wanted to see us off at the car—and now we were about to leave. I was glad the Addis curfew was midnight, for although it was getting very dark, we could still legally be abroad. We carried a transistor radio, a flashlight, and the food cooler out to my sturdy Mercedes and put them into the trunk.

Lali and Bete' climbed in, chatting happily. Deme and I went back to the living room, where Mickey was waiting. He looked so thin! I wrapped a *gabby* around his frail shoulders, and then Deme gripped his arm and the two walked down the steps to Assafa's waiting hand. I followed and was about to get into the car when I stopped.

I suddenly *had* to go back inside that house. Something was happening to me that made no sense.

"I'll be back in a moment," I said. I ran up the steps. As I entered the hall, I saw a roll of electrical tape on one of the chairs. Why was it there? Normally we kept the house free of clutter and I hadn't seen the tape earlier. I reached for it and put it into my purse. What a strange thing to do!

Then I turned left and went into the living room. In front of me on a corner table was a picture of His Majesty. He was standing in front of his throne and looking beyond the camera in his usual serious way. I picked up the portrait to study the face of the man I had so greatly respected. As I did so I realized that very soon now, when soldiers came to seal the house, they would throw the picture to the floor. I wanted to take it with me, but I couldn't just walk out with it in my hand. Could I wrap it up? I saw the blue-and-white embroidered cloth that Madame Tito had given me years ago. I took it off of the table and wrapped it around the portrait of His Majesty.

Then, still on this mysterious errand, with my family waiting outside, another unexplainable urge came over me. I stepped onto the veranda and called down to the boys.

"Did any of you think to pack Vaseline? You'll need it for your skin."

Bete' answered, "No, we didn't."

"Well, come back up, please. I saw a jar on the shelf in your room. Will you get it?"

Bete' got out of the car and cheerfully raced up the steps, as I walked back down to the car. I almost wished Assafa were not waiting to say goodbye to us. I made a special point of trying to appear calm, but I also told him how pleased we had always been with him. I knew he would remember those words when he heard of our escape and would know that we had tried to tell him goodbye.

Bete' came running back down the steps, handed me the jar of Vaseline, and jumped into the back seat. I put the jar into my too-crowded purse, adjusted a little gold-colored cushion at my back, and settled the wrapped portrait of His Majesty in my lap. Finally, smiling and waving at Assafa, Deme put the car into gear, and we drove away from our home of so many years, away from the house where my mother had died, away . . . away from Father, who was praying for us even now in his room.

At the top of the hill we were stopped by the lowered

military barrier. Several new soldiers stood in a circle of lights, their rifles in the ready position. "Please Lord, let us through."

The soldier nearest our car leaned down. How young he was! Not even as old as our 22-year-old Mickey. To our suprise he smiled as he asked for our identifications.

"You folks are out a little late, aren't you? Where are you headed?"

"Toward Lake Langano," Deme said quickly. That was true enough; the youth didn't catch the evasion.

"Well," said the soldier, handing back Deme's papers, "be sure to be out of the city by midnight." The midnight curfew did not extend to the countryside, just to the city proper.

"Thank you," said Deme.

The soldier stepped aside and signaled to the posthouse for the barrier to be raised.

"Thank You, Lord," Deme and I both whispered as our car passed under the gate. Even as I thanked God for getting us through the first barrier I was asking Him also to take us safely to the little farming community outside Addis where we were supposed to meet the Land Rover.

The fifteen kilometers to the rendezvous point seemed unbearably long. I watched our headlights pierce the darkness. The boys chatted lazily in the back seat. Occasionally I could see distant, dim lights from farmers' adobe houses on the hillsides, but I could not make out the mountains that I had enjoyed since my childhood.

At last Deme slowed down. We began to look into the fields by the side of the road for the big acacia tree where the Land Rover was supposed to be waiting. Finally the tree loomed ahead of us out of the darkness. But the Land Rover wasn't there!

Deme slowed almost to a halt. The road at that point was little more than one lane wide. On both sides were fields. I saw no lights from nearby houses. What should we do? The boys were sure to ask questions if we simply stopped. For their peace of mind our plan was still not to speak about the escape until we had to.

Suddenly the car began to jerk. I looked at Deme in the darkness and could just make out in the instrument lights' soft glow that his foot was hitting the accelerator to make the car buck.

"What's the trouble?" I asked, my voice loud and clear.

"I'll take a look," Deme answered.

He pulled the car over by the acacia tree. Mickey, though his voice was weak, kept up a word game with his brothers. Deme raised the hood and tinkered for a while, and then closed it and got back into the car. "Let's try again," he said and started down the road. The boys had never stopped their game.

Suddenly taillights appeared ahead of us. "That's a Land Rover," Deme said. How could he tell just from the taillights? Deme drove faster in order to catch them. As he was passing he waved, then pulled to the side of the road. The Land Rover followed. Deme got out of our car.

"Why are we stopped?" Bete' asked. "Where's Dad going?"

I answered with a, "Shhh. It's some men he needs to talk to." Inwardly I was praying, *Please, Lord, just seal our sons' lips. Help them not to ask questions that will be dangerous for me to answer.*

I watched Deme in the darkness. He was walking around to the back of the Land Rover, as though checking to make sure no one else was in the vehicle. We were becoming unnaturally suspicious in all of this, but these men had already changed the plans several times. Had they decided something different now or were we going to get into the Land Rover?

Then I had still another strange experience. I knew something was wrong! We should not get into that vehicle, at least not here. Maybe someone was watching? Whatever the reason, I knew we were to wait before we got into the Land Rover. Then Deme came back to the car and opened the door. "They're ready," he said.

I kept my voice at a whisper. "Deme, would it be all right if we drove on a bit further? Something isn't right."

In the pale light from the car's interior, he looked relieved. "Yes. That is my feeling, too. This is of the Lord."

Quickly he turned back to tell Rebe that we would meet them beyond Mojo, a village just a few kilometers ahead. Rebe argued for a moment, but with a shrug he finally agreed.

Rebe told Deme he would follow in about ten minutes. We pulled back onto the road.

Mickey quickly picked up the word game until we reached Mojo. Suddenly we came to a military barrier across the road! I glanced at the car clock: there was plenty of time before the curfew and besides, we were well out of Addis. But what was the new, unexpected barrier doing here?

Deme stopped.

The soldier leaned down to ask for our identification. He shone his flashlight into the car. I spread my coat over the cloth-covered picture of His Majesty. Did the soldier notice that my hands were shaking? He moved back. "Go ahead."

Both Deme and I let out our breath. But before we could comment a policeman appeared in our headlights and put up his hand for us to stop.

My hands really shook now! It was clear that the guard had changed his mind about letting us pass. The policeman coming toward us was strong-looking and carried a sidearm.

While our car rolled toward him, Deme said, "Let's pretend we don't see him."

Then I did something that I knew I shouldn't do in front of our sons—I contradicted Deme. "No. Stop."

We were exchanging these words while the car was slowing. Certainly the policeman had the authority to shoot at us if we didn't stop.

Quickly he came over to Deme's window. "I need a ride," he said.

We were startled by the demand. Deme hesitated, but just as impulsively as I had previously contradicted my husband I now said, in what I hoped was a bright voice, "Sure! Boys, scoot over."

The policeman opened the back door of the Mercedes and got in. As Deme accelerated I casually tucked my coat around His Majesty's picture and then turned sideways to talk to the policeman. I chatted about the weather, and had just asked him about his family when, apropos of nothing, he said:

"Where are you folks headed?"

The question jolted me. I was trying to think of an answer when the policeman suddenly called out, "Oh, this is it. Stop! I almost missed my house."

Deme slammed on the brakes so quickly that the car swerved. The policeman pointed out his window in the darkness. "Yes, there's my place."

He got out of the car, calling a quick "Thanks" over his shoulder as he hurried off. Deme and I looked at each other in the dim light. Now we knew why we had had to drive this little bit farther in our Mercedes, with the Land Rover following. Not only did we have to pass that unexpected barrier, but how would we have explained to the policeman our back compartment of a Land Rover filled with four people and gasoline for a long trip? I whispered, "Thank You, Lord."

How many more of these unexpected turns were waiting for us?

A few minutes later we arrived at the place where Rebe had promised to meet us. Deme stopped and once again got out and raised the hood. He pretended to be examining the engine for trouble. The moon had lost its cloud cover, but in the space between the car and the raised hood I could just make out Deme's hand touching various parts of the engine.

Where was that Land Rover? Fresh doubts flooded over me until I had to squeeze my eyes shut and silently pray. *I know this fear is not of You, Lord. But still all these thoughts rush toward me. Take away the doubts. And, please, have Rebe get here soon.*

When I opened my eyes, I turned toward my sons to make sure Mickey had his *gabby* wrapped tightly around his shoul-

85

ders. Lali was asleep, his breathing peaceful. Mickey and Bete' looked questioningly at me, but I could think of nothing to say. It occurred to me that perhaps by now they were both acting along with Deme and me, for security's sake.

I turned back toward Deme. He was watching headlights approaching us in the distance. My heart raced. Within moments, the lights pulled up behind our car and for a few seconds I was blinded. Then I heard Wolde's unpleasant, guttural voice.

I became extremely nervous. As I opened my door, I said to the boys, "Get out. Get out."

Bete' shook Lali awake and almost carried his groggy brother out. Mickey got out, too, wrapping his *gabby* tightly about his shoulders. The three boys stood by our car. Clutching my purse and the little cushion in one hand and His Majesty's picture with the other, I managed to gesture toward the vehicle. "Get into the back of the Land Rover. Hurry! Hurry!"

Why was I surprised that none of them asked any questions? Hadn't I asked the Lord to seal their lips? "Hurry!" I said again.

Bete' and Lali helped Mickey climb up into the Land Rover, and then climbed in after him while Deme and the other men transferred our gear from the car trunk to the Land Rover.

The canvas covering for the vehicle looked flimsy in the moonlight. Lemma climbed aboard. Rebe shone his flashlight inside. My three sons and Lemma were safely positioned next to a 50-gallon drum of gasoline and the suitcases and the cooler. The back was terribly crowded, but still not one of the boys questioned what we were doing. Had they all known, perhaps right from the beginning? My eyes filled with tears as I realized that this might be true. They'd heard of other attempted escapes. Maybe each was trying to protect the others!

"Let's go!" said Wolde.

Deme handed him the keys to the Mercedes. Without another syllable Wolde got into my car and drove into the night. I felt no sadness as I watched my old black car being driven away. Rebe hurried around to the driver's side of the Land

Rover. Deme opened the other door and helped me in. Then he was next to me, squeezing my hand and again whispering, "Thank You, Lord."

Monday, September 1. Ten minutes past midnight—four hours after leaving home.

I turned around, peering through the window between us and the cargo compartment, but it was too dark to see the boys and Lemma. Rebe, Deme and I did not talk. We were too intent on looking into the night. We continued to drive through the darkness and past farming villages. Each kilometer took us that much farther from Addis toward the safety waiting for us beyond the Kenyan desert.

Then, just before 1:00 a.m.—five hours away from home—the Land Rover stalled.

Immediately Rebe threw the gear into neutral and turned the key again as he muttered a low curse.

"What's wrong?" Deme asked.

"I don't know," Rebe grunted. He turned the key again. All he got was a grinding sound. "Come on, come on," he pleaded. He turned the key again as the vehicle coasted along the asphalt.

That time it backfired . . . and caught. Only then did I realize how tightly I had been gripping Deme's arm.

But just as we let out our breath, the engine stalled again. This time Rebe brought the Land Rover to a stop beside the road. We all got out. Deme and Rebe opened the hood. Lemma jumped out of the back compartment with the flashlight. Bete' helped his brothers out. Lali leaned into my arms and I hugged him.

"Where are we?" Lali asked.

"Not yet to Arbaminch," I answered numbly. No other questions were asked. Yes, they knew.

I walked up to the front of the vehicle to see what was wrong. I stood next to Deme as he shone the light in at the engine.

Quickly I asked, "What is it?"

Deme shook his head in annoyance. "Why didn't I check this engine myself? Why did I accept Wolde's word that it was O.K.? Look at that."

I leaned forward to look into the nest of engine parts, but all I saw were oily metal shapes and dirty hoses. "Oh," I said. "Can you fix it?"

"I don't know. It's the fuel pump."

I walked away quickly to keep from adding my anger to Deme's. Repeated delays, broken appointments, a driver and a guide who knew nothing about the condition of their vehicle. Deme was totally in charge. It was up to him to figure out some way to fix the fuel pump.

"Please, Lord," I prayed aloud, "show Deme what to do. Please don't let us get caught out here."

I walked back to the boys, but I didn't know what to say other than, "It'll be all right." I stood with them, my hands on Lali's shoulders as he leaned against me, and watched the road for headlights.

After what seemed like endless hours—in actuality it was only about 30 minutes—Deme came back to us.

"It's fixed. At least for now. We'll fill the gas tank and be on our way."

I gave Lali a thankful hug as we watched the men roll the gasoline drum to the back and drain off what was needed. In a few minutes we were moving hesitantly down the road.

We drove slowly for an hour, listening to every unusual sound from the engine. Suddenly the vehicle stalled again. There was nothing to do but get out and repeat the earlier process.

Before I could get back into the Land Rover, Deme led me a little distance away from the others.

"Marta, we can't keep this up. That fuel pump will never get us through the desert. We'll have to get it repaired."

I stared into the shadows that hid his face from me. When I didn't reply Deme spoke again. "If we get caught down here, they'll know we are escaping. We'll have to go all the way back up to Nazareth."

"Nazareth? But that's so far out of our way!"

"All the better. If we get caught there we can say we are going to Dire Dawa. The soldiers will believe us since Nazareth is on the way to the business."

My sigh was my answer. Soon we were heading north along the same route we had traveled just a short time before. Along the way, the engine stalled several more times. Deme was right; we would never have made it through the desert.

Monday, September 1. Dawn in Addis Ababa.

Unknown to us, at this hour two military vehicles pulled up to our home in Addis Ababa. When a startled Assafa told the lieutenant we had left for a holiday, one of the vehicles was dispatched to follow us. The other soldiers stayed behind to seal the house, after ordering Assafa and the other household staff out. Father remained in his own home.

It was dawn when we reached Nazareth. Totally surrounded by the beautiful mountains of the highlands, the town seemed to sit in the bottom of a great earthen teacup. Just as we entered the town, the Land Rover backfired and stalled again—this time almost in front of a hotel. Deme and I looked at each other, our eyes expressing our thankfulness. Now the challenge was to get the vehicle repaired without giving our situation away. I tried not to think that we had left our home ten hours earlier and were no farther along than Nazareth.

A party of seven walking bag and baggage into a hotel at dawn was unusual enough for us to feel terribly conspicuous. We tried not to be paranoid, but I'm afraid we were. We decided not to buy food or eat in the hotel while we were in Nazareth, for fear of being recognized. I later remembered that decision with regret.

Once we were in our rooms, the cooler yielded breakfast for the others, but neither Deme nor I took anything. Without discussing it, both of us had decided we would not eat until we were safely across the border.

When the boys had eaten, Deme and I insisted they go to

bed and not leave their rooms for any reason. Then we sat down to plan our next step. We needed two things—someone to get gasoline for us, and a garage where we could get the fuel pump repaired.

It was then that we remembered Ben, an old friend who lived in Nazareth. He was our only hope. With some difficulty Deme was able to get the Land Rover started again and we drove to Ben's house. Ben, always an early riser, must have seen us pull into his yard because he came running out almost immediately, rubbing his hand over his bald head in delight. After cheerful greetings, we told him that we needed to find a garage that was open at this early hour. He looked at the Land Rover and then back at us, but didn't ask questions.

"There's an Italian mechanic near here," he said. And then he lowered his voice to a whisper. "But we all have to be careful. There are spies everywhere."

His statement startled me, and I wondered if our plans were that obvious! I decided to come right to the point.

"Ben, we need gasoline too."

He nodded slowly. "Yes, I'll get you some from my storage area. But when you are talking to the mechanic, don't mention me. And be very careful of his wife."

At the garage I stood listening to Deme explain, in that strange mechanic's language of his, exactly what he had done to the fuel pump to get us started. Suddenly I realized I was being watched.

The Italian's wife had come from their house adjacent to the garage and seemed all too interested in what was going on. She was a tall, heavy woman in her late fifties who watched everything with her hands on her hips. I wanted to get her away from the Land Rover.

As I approached her, I realized this was going to be a battle of wits. Abruptly I began, "You know, I'm just amazed that you don't offer coffee to your guests."

She was so startled at my rudeness that she suddenly lost

her frown. She hooked a loose strand of hair back over one ear and said, "There's some hot. I'll be right back."

To have her come right back was exactly what I didn't want, so I followed her. But almost instantly I was sorry I had done so. As soon as she poured the coffee, she began testing me.

"Do you know that man Zelke?" she asked. I was suddenly alert. She continued, "The one who made those radio speeches?" She was probing for a reaction.

I shrugged. "Yes, I heard him speak. What about him?"

She grinned. "Well, they arrested him!" She was watching me closely; I had to have my wits about me.

"Oh?"

"Yes, they got him while he was trying to escape."

My heart stopped. That simply wasn't true. Gera had always been right, hadn't she? She had said Zelke had been arrested at his office. I made no comment, but yawned and started to rise. The woman, with a flash of insistence, gestured for me to sit down as she spoke again.

It was important to appear relaxed so I stirred my coffee. *Please, Lord,* I said inwardly.

The woman continued. "They arrested one of their own men, isn't that something?"

I stirred my drink, while the woman tried another tactic. "He was a good man, but he had it coming."

I ignored the contradiction and concentrated on a piece of lint on my slacks. She continued, "Yes, he was a wealthy man. No one should have more than what he needs. The Communists came to lift us up and help us. No one should be sorry for the rich who are destroyed."

I asked a question of my own. "What about you? Your husband is a businessman. Are you safe?"

She laughed. "Yes, we're safe. Besides, we're poor. The Communists will help us. Don't worry, we are *quite* safe."

I wanted to get out of there as fast as possible. "If you will excuse me," I said, "I'll go see if your good husband has been able to fix our vehicle."

91

I was encouraged by the fact that she didn't seem interested enough to follow. And I breathed thanks to the Lord for His having allowed me to pull it off.

Deme was standing by the Land Rover when I entered the garage. He motioned for me to join him outside. "We ordered a new fuel pump, but it won't be here until tomorrow. We'll have to stay over. The Italian can work on it in the morning."

"Oh, Deme. We should be so far along by now. Instead, here we are, sitting under the very noses of the Committee."

He said simply, "I know."

Tuesday, 8:00 a.m. We had been in Nazareth over 24 hours.

I wondered if the word was out that we had left Addis Ababa. If so, the Committee's soldiers would be looking for us. Perhaps they had already sent out a general alert for our capture.

As the new fuel pump was being installed, I thought about going shopping for food, but I was afraid people would notice me. Even though we were still many hours from the border it seemed better to lie low. As we started out again, the frustration of delay was overwhelming.

"Lord," I said in a whisper as we pulled out of Nazareth, "we're having to travel by daylight. Help me to relax into Your arms. So far You have overruled every obstacle. But why? When we're out of Ethiopia, what do You want us to do?"

Chapter Nine

Tuesday, 3:00 p.m. Six hours beyond Nazareth.

When we were a few kilometers from Arbaminch, the town that was full of hostile students, we pulled off the road to wait until around five o'clock. We wanted to go through town in the middle of the busy hour when the students would be concentrating on getting home.

As we waited beneath some acacia trees in a grassy field, I passed food around. I used the aluminum foil that the chicken had been wrapped in as a serving tray, and then tossed it back into the cooler.

With a piece of chicken in his hand, Rebe spread the map across the hood of the Land Rover.

"If we get past the Arbaminch market safely, we will be heading into the most dangerous part of the town. The police station will be on our right and the school will be across the street. The students are radicals and very dangerous."

"Rebe," I asked, "why don't we go around the town if it's so risky?"

He nodded. "There are deep ditches out there, remember?" he said, pointing left and right of the highway. He turned to Lemma. "Rest," he said. "We'll leave at five."

Deme motioned for me to join him under a nearby tree. He positioned my little gold-colored cushion against the trunk. Then he sat next to me, took my hand in his, and prayed aloud. "Lord, we thank You that we have come this far and we ask that You take us through Arbaminch. You know that it is a critical spot and that much could happen. Please be with us."

Finally we had to go.

For the first time Lali and Bete' were slow getting into the Land Rover.

"What's the matter, boys?" Deme asked.

Lali looked at the ground. Bete' kicked a rock. It was Mickey, looking more pallid and frail then ever, who spoke for them.

"They heard Rebe and Lemma talking about an escaping family who were caught in this town."

I looked at Deme. None of us had openly admitted our flight. There was an unspoken agreement that we would not discuss what was happening, just as I understand families escaping Nazi Germany under the guise of taking a holiday often kept up the pretense among themselves until they were safe. I was furious at Rebe and Lemma, yet I did not want to add to the tension by fighting with them.

In the end I could do nothing but hug each of my sons in turn. I held them to me, trying to pass on to them a confidence I myself did not feel.

"Let's go," said Rebe.

I gave Lali an extra hug as I handed him up into the arms of his teenage brother. Then Mickey pulled himself up into the back, his orange skin frightening me. "Mickey," I said, "make sure you drink some water."

It never occurred to me to ration the water.

As we drove through the fading light toward Arbaminch, Rebe was peering into the twilight. "I don't want to turn on my lights. That might call attention to us."

Ahead of us adobe houses began to emerge out of the dusk. As we approached, we could see a group of children playing in the road. Suddenly one of the boys punched his friend and then darted away—right into the path of the Land Rover! Rebe swerved in time to miss the child, but without another word he turned on his headlights.

We arrived in Arbaminch at dusk. As Rebe had predicted, the streets were filled with people on their way home, so no one watched us as we drove through the market area. Ahead of us now was the police station, on our right, just as Rebe had said. The school was on our left.

Rebe sucked in his breath as we saw a crowd of students in front of the school, apparently just dismissed from a late meeting. We would be going within a foot of that group! Closest to the road were five or six tall young men in agitated conversation.

Just as the Land Rover started to pass the group, one of the young men pushed another one. He knocked against our side-view mirror and broke it, fell to the ground for an instant, then jumped up. Rebe froze.

The Land Rover began to slow down.

Deme almost shouted. "Don't stop! Don't stop!"

A pack of the students started to come toward us as our vehicle moved away from the young man, who was shaking his fist at us. Rebe was still stunned. In his hysterical state he cried, "It won't go! It won't go!"

Quickly Deme stomped his own foot on top of Rebe's. The accelerator pressed to the floor.

As the Land Rover jumped forward, I looked back past Lemma and the alarmed boys, huddled together, and in the twilight I saw the student who had fallen being examined by his friends. Another student ran toward the police station. Others shouted and gestured toward us. Deme turned around, too.

"He's all right. Now go on. Go on!"

Finally Rebe was in control of himself again. "Thank You, Lord," I said. How soon would the police start looking for the Land Rover that had raced away from the students?

"Are you boys all right?" I asked. All three mumbled something. I had to turn back around. The highway outside Arbaminch wasn't paved and Rebe was driving fast over the uneven dirt road. Bouncing along, we kept trying to look behind us to see if any lights were coming. Suddenly Lemma shouted from the rear, "That's them! Volkswagen lights just appeared!"

I looked back and saw headlights that seemed to be gaining on us. Police in that area drove Volkswagens. Suddenly there was a terrible bouncing. I turned back just in time to see us heading into a dark field. "What are we doing?" I managed to gasp.

Rebe shut off our lights. Between teeth-rattling bounces he answered, "There's heavy bush just to the southeast. We'll hide there."

"What about those ditches?" Deme asked.

"We'll just have to chance it."

We were crossing a field filled with large rocks that constantly loomed up out of the dark. Rebe had to keep turning the wheel quickly to avoid hitting them. Branches from a bush ripped open the canvas over the back compartment. The boys and Lemma must have been freezing! Cold night air rushed through the jammed-open window between the cab and the cargo area, sweeping across my shoulders and neck.

Suddenly we stopped. Ahead of us was a large gully.

Deme and Rebe got out to look at it with shielded flashlight. They returned, shaking their heads. There was no way to cross the ditch, they said. We would have to wait here.

We sat in the dark field for four hours. I kept trying to reassure the boys, especially little Lali. But he was a bright ten-year-old, and he asked me why, if everything was all right now, was I whispering?

Finally Deme decided it was safe to get back to the road. But now, in addition to the worry about the police, we were also suffering from the cold air that was coming into the vehicle. Almost to himself, Deme muttered, "If only we had something to secure that canvas with."

Then I remembered the electrical tape I had picked up, without knowing why, in the hallway at home. "Oh, yes! We do have something!"

When I brought the tape out of my purse, both Rebe and Deme were thrilled. Immediately we pulled off the road into another field so that, using the flashlight in the dark, they could repair the rip. As they climbed back into the vehicle Rebe said, "What a smart thing, to think of bringing tape!"

"But I didn't think of it. The Lord had me pick it up."

In the darkness Deme took my hand to show his under-standing, but Rebe grunted a retort. "Do you really think Allah is interested in providing such things for a journey?"

I leaned my head against Deme's shoulder and replied softly, "The Lord is watching over us."

Wednesday, 6:00 a.m. Dawn. We should have arrived in Marsabit yesterday.

As the sun started to rise, I was wondering how much farther we had to go before we came to the desert. Rebe spoke.

"We'll have to stay off the road today. They patrol this area heavily."

So last night's four-hour delay was going to cost us a whole day's travel time. I knew we had just enough food for a few mouthfuls. Where could I buy more?

We pulled well off the road into a cluster of thorn trees and spreading acacias. I walked to the back to tell the boys to do some stretching exercises. Here it was Wednesday morning. They had been traveling in cramped quarters all Sunday night and again since we had left Nazareth Tuesday morning. How tired they looked, especially poor Mickey! They had not eaten since yesterday when I gave them half-sandwiches.

I opened the cooler and picked up the bit of cheese remain-ing and a few slices of the bread. Very carefully I broke the bread into five small pieces so everyone could see we were out of food; I couldn't bring myself to tell them. There was also a bite of cheese to go with the bread. I said to myself, *That will have to last until we get to Marsabit tonight.*

When they all had finished their meager meal, I carefully poured a few thimblefuls of water into each of the crystal glasses the cook had packed. After that there were two good drinks of water left and Mickey needed more than that just for himself!

I collected the glasses, wrapped them in the paper towels again and put them next to the empty tomato juice cans in the cooler. I noticed the foil that I hadn't thrown away, either.

97

What use would we have for the tin cans and foil? But I left both in the cooler, too tired to reason why.

I walked over to Rebe, Deme and Lemma who were looking at the map. Rebe pointed to the area south of Arbaminch.

"O.K., now this is where we are. And here is Yabelo." He pointed with his cigarette to a town still further south. "When it gets dark, we'll *try* to go through the dry riverbed to bypass the road crew at Yabelo. I don't want to be seen by that crew! They caught a family last month and turned them over to the police."

"Keep your voice down, will you?" I said, annoyed that he was repeating this story within earshot of my sons. Into my mind flashed the image of the bullet-riddled bodies we had been shown on television.

Rebe continued in a lower voice, pointing again to the map. "Then after Yabelo there's Mega. We'll have to go around Mega, too, if we can. That's where all the police are. We'll try to detour the outpost by going through the sand dunes. Then it's over the border, across the desert, and into Marsabit by midmorning."

He made it sound so easy.

The rest of that Wednesday afternoon we just sat waiting for the time when we could safely leave for our attempted detour of Yabelo. We were too tired to talk. Deme and I leaned against an acacia tree and looked at the sky. How peaceful the scene was! I closed my eyes and asked the Lord to continue to be with us throughout the coming night.

But as I prayed, I suddenly knew we were not going to make it into Kenya so soon. I wondered if trouble would come from soldiers or if something was ahead that we weren't counting on. Either way, safety was still far off.

My hands had been folded in my lap, but I let them fall to my side as I mouthed the words, "Please help us, Lord Jesus."

How can I explain the rush of comfort that surrounded me then? I couldn't form my prayer into more than those few words, and yet I was experiencing peace. Into my mind flowed promises from the Bible—"I will never leave thee nor forsake thee," and, "He careth for you," and, "Therefore do not be anxious."

I was still sitting with my eyes closed, still drawing help from the verses that were stored in my memory, when Deme touched my arm. "Marta, it's time to go."

I stood up, strangely refreshed. Whatever trouble was ahead was under the control of the Father. Our responsibility was to do what we could and leave the outcome to Him.

Wednesday, 6:00 p.m. Three days after leaving Addis.

The detour that would, we hoped, allow us to bypass that road crew at Yabelo was little more than a donkey trail. The single track led toward a riverbed that we could just make out in the distance. It was rough going in the gathering darkness. A Land Rover in good condition would have taken a beating over that bumpy path. What damage would the jolting do to *our* vehicle?

Twenty minutes later, our headlights were dropping down into the riverbed. Rebe kept making under-the-breath comments about the steepness of the bank. There was little rain in this area, so the riverbed was dry. As we lurched down the bank and started up the riverbed I was startled by the size of the boulders around us. Rebe steered around the largest ones but often there was nothing to do but climb over the rocks.

I held my breath with each shifting bounce. It was teeth-rattling. We couldn't talk. I was worried about the gasoline in the back. What if the drum fell over?

After one especially severe bump, I managed a question. "The gasoline . . . drum?"

Rebe answered. "Lemma's feet . . . against it." Each word had been punctuated by another rocking bounce.

The lights of the Land Rover ricocheted from boulder to boulder, and I wondered how much longer our vehicle could take the punishment. And the noise! Surely if there were families living in this area they could hear the grinding of the gears and the scraping of the undercarriage against the rocks. Would they come out of their little round-roofed houses to watch the bobbing lights in the riverbed? Would they know someone was trying to escape? Would they understand why?

In the darkness I could barely see Rebe, but it seemed to me he was pulling at the steering wheel with increased force. I wondered if something was wrong but didn't want to ask. I gripped Deme's hand as I silently prayed that we would soon be out of that awful place.

Suddenly, after yet another jolt, Rebe pulled to a stop. "We've got problems."

We all got out, and were immediately inundated by hordes of insects! They were all over us—buzzing in our ears, darting into our nostrils, at our eyes, down into our throats as we tried to breathe. "Come on, boys!" I said, trying to cover myself and my sons with a *gabby*. It was useless.

Deme, slapping at his face, shone his flashlight around the vehicle. His light was dimmed by the thousands of insects. The creatures were in my hair and on the backs of my hands. There was no protection. I put the *gabby* back, continuing to slap at the biting plague. I could feel their stings through my clothing as they poured over my back and legs.

Deme kept wiping the insects off the flashlight and shining it toward the wheel. Each time he would have just a few seconds of light before it was darkened again. We could see that the wheel was wedged awkwardly against a rock, as though it had pulled away from the vehicle.

"Deme, what's wrong?"

Deme's voice was muffled. He had his hand over his mouth to keep the insects out of his throat. "The nuts have jolted loose. The threads are stripped."

I didn't know what that meant. All I understood was that we were in trouble. Through my hand I asked, "What can you do?"

His muffled voice came out of the buzzing darkness. "We'll have to put the wheel back on. We must find those nuts."

He wiped off the insects and tried to shine the light onto the ground. How could we ever find the nuts in the dark in a riverbed and with a million swarming insects blinding us?

"Come on, boys. Come on, Lemma," said Deme. "We have to try!"

All seven of us—even Mickey—began to pat the ground with our hands, hoping.

But the insects! "Isn't there any relief from them?" I moaned as I slapped at my face and hair.

For perhaps ten minutes we swatted at the insects and felt for the nuts along the dirt between the boulders. Finally Deme's muffled voice came through the buzzing.

"It's no use. They must have bounced off one by one. But I have an idea. Maybe we can take two nuts from the other wheels."

He walked back to the Land Rover. I stumbled after him. "We need the wrenches," Deme called to Lemma. "The tool case is behind the food chest."

We waited for several minutes, slapping at the droning insects and listening to the sounds of the search for the tool case. Finally the back of the vehicle opened.

"It's not here!" Lemma said.

Not there! Deme jumped in to check for himself. After several minutes he gave up.

"The Italian was using those tools in Nazareth," he said. "Well, let's hope there's a wrench in this vehicle somewhere. We must have one."

Lali and Bete' climbed back into the rear compartment to see if they could find a tool, and Mickey and the men searched the cab, while I stood outside and prayed. "Lord, we need a miracle. Thank You for the tool You have already provided. Now please help us find it."

Long agonizing minutes passed. Then I heard a shout. It

was Mickey's voice. "Look," he called. "A wrench! I found a wrench under the seat!"

As the insects buzzed around my mouth and nose, I whispered my gratitude to the Lord.

The men worked for several minutes, getting rusted nuts off the back wheels, still slapping helplessly at the insects. When they discovered that we also had no jack we all, including the little boys, *lifted* the front of the Land Rover while Mickey put the nuts on. I began to hope we'd make it out after all.

Thursday. Just before dawn of our fourth day on the road.
The sky was barely beginning to lighten in the east when we finally faced the reality of our bad news. We were not going to be able to bypass Yabelo. The riverbed had finally become impassable with boulders and ditches. We would have to go back to the main road and drive right through Yabelo!

"All right," said Rebe, "we might as well take advantage of every little thing we have going for us. It's just before dawn, when people sleep their soundest. There is a rise in the road at Yabelo. Perhaps we can simply *coast* through town."

"It's worth a try," Deme said.

So, praying for still one more protection, we struggled as silently as possible back to the main highway and on to within a kilometer of Yabelo.

Rebe turned off his lights. He pulled to a stop on a slight rise well outside the village. Buildings, just visible up ahead, seemed heavy and black, forbidding. I wondered which ones belonged to the road crew.

"I'll get going fast, then cut the engine," Rebe said.

He began to move again, picking up speed until I wondered how our wheels could stay on. Chill, pre-dawn air whistled through the cab. We held on. Then, abruptly, Rebe threw out the clutch, slipped the Land Rover into neutral and put his finger to his mouth for silence. The motor died. The vehicle sped forward down the gradual incline. Our tires seemed to me to be making an enormous uproar, but doubtless we were just a whisper as we rolled over bits of sand and gravel on the road.

The Land Rover was inside the village now. Dark houses sat, ominous and threatening, on either side of us. In some of them, I knew, lived men capable of turning in families like our own. I strained my eyes for lights shining behind shutters. Nothing.

In the near-silent darkness my hand sought Deme's. He squeezed back a prayer. The vehicle was slowing now and we were still inside the village. Come on, come on!

Up ahead I could make out what appeared to be garages. The highway department! We rolled, ghostlike, past the rank of Land Rovers used by the state work crews. Nothing. Not one movement.

We were coasting still more slowly now but we had passed the highway department and were approaching the last of the dark hulks of houses and shops that were the hamlet of Yabelo. *Thank You, Lord.*

Now our tires whispered very, *very* softly. We'd almost stopped.

The last of the buildings was behind us. I turned around and tried to peer through the rear cab window, out through the cargo opening. No sign of life.

The vehicle edged slower, slower through the pre-dawn. To our left the first signs of light appeared. I could make out Rebe's hand moving now toward the ignition switch. Just before the vehicle came to a stop he put it into gear again, and a click in the darkness was followed by a soft grinding, and then our engine fired. Rebe let out the clutch. We moved forward.

Well away from Yabelo, Rebe pulled off to the side of the road. In the light of full dawn, to our left, I could see Rebe's hands. They were shaking. I looked at Deme and we smiled. Our hand-squeeze prayer had been answered.

Thursday. Just after sunup of the fourth day.

Half-an-hour out of Yabelo, when we stopped by the road-side to tighten the nuts once again, it was clear that Rebe had not calmed down. A private car sped by in the early morning light, the passengers staring at us but not—thank God—offering help. Rebe looked at the nuts and bolts on the wheel nearest him and shook his head.

"I don't like it," he said. "This area is heavily patrolled." He reached into his shirt pocket and pulled out the now dog-eared map and spread it out on the hood. Rebe's none-too-steady finger jabbed at the next danger spot on our route, Mega, where the police force had recently been doubled. "We shouldn't be out here on this road in daylight. Too near Mega. I'd hate to try to outrun a patrol with this thing!" He spat at the wheel.

So we decided to get off the main road again. Rebe spotted a heavy growth of acacia trees in the distance and we took off cross-country toward them. The grove was extensive, a minia-ture, low-growing forest well out of sight from the main road. Everything looked alike—the acacia trees, the rocks, the gullies. I was glad the sun was still low in the morning sky; otherwise I'd be even more disoriented!

The men were once more worrying those nuts and bolts on our wheels, trying to get them to fit more tightly. As the sun rose higher it was obvious that Rebe was becoming more and more frustrated. "Look," he said at last, "if we want to go over sand dunes to get around the police at Mega, we'll have to do better than this." He kicked the front wheel. "I have a friend who has a garage near here. Why don't Lemma and I get him to *weld* that front wheel on?"

It seemed like a good idea. So we drove a little further until we found an especially large acacia tree, offering some relief from the sun, and there we unloaded the Land Rover in case Rebe and Lemma were searched. Out came the gasoline drum and the food chest, the luggage and the portrait of His Majes-ty. I spread the blanket for our weary sons and told them to

104

stretch out. The three collapsed without comment. How tired they looked from their many hours cramped together in the back compartment.

Deme and I watched the Land Rover bounce away and then settled down near the boys, who were trying to sleep.

"Is there any water, Mom?" Mickey asked.

I opened the chest, took out the last bottle and held it up. There was just enough for a couple of good swallows. The conversation aroused Lali and Bete' and they wanted a drink, too. I pulled out the surviving crystal glasses (there were only three left unbroken), divided the water and gave it to my sons.

The food had run out yesterday.

And now the water was gone.

Chapter Ten

Thursday, 10:00 a.m. of the fourth day.

Had the soldiers followed the main highway all the way into Kenya without finding us? Assuming that we had not yet left the country, had they sent an order for our arrest to all police outposts, including the one we were trying to go around at Mega?

An hour went by. Two. We began to worry. Three hours passed. Something had gone seriously wrong. We decided to walk toward the place we had last seen the Land Rover.

Putting our gear into a ditch near our large acacia tree, the three boys and Deme and I stumbled through the matted grass. After just a few moments, the boys began falling behind, so Deme insisted that the four of us wait for him while he walked on. I was too weary to argue.

The three boys and I sat close together beneath another acacia. Lali and Bete' put their heads on my lap while Mickey leaned against my shoulder. Was it my imagination, or was Mickey's skin not quite the shade of orange it had been?

All three of the boys were listless, their grimy faces showing the trauma of the last four days. Their lips were parched and beginning to crack.

While we waited, I said things like, "Be strong," and, "The Lord is with us. Remember how He gave us the wrench last night? He is with us here, too."

Finally I became impatient. "Come on, boys. Let's try again. I know you can walk just a little more."

Just then in the distance, through the acacias, a cloud of dust began to move toward us. It was our Land Rover! Deme and Rebe and Lemma were all safe!

"What happened?" we shouted as the vehicle pulled up. "Where have you been? Did he fix it?"

Deme spoke quietly. "The wheel is *sort of* fixed. But we can't move now. We saw police vehicles everywhere in the distance. Let's fill up with gas and find a place to hide until dark."

So we started back for the acacia tree where we had left our gear and the gasoline. But then a horrible thing happened! All of the acacias suddenly looked alike. *We couldn't find the tree where we had left the gasoline!* Every time one of us said, "There it is!" we would hurry on, only to discover it wasn't our tree after all.

In desperation I literally dropped to my knees, my hands imploringly raised toward heaven. "Lord, please help us remember where we left the gasoline. We are tired and confused. Guide us."

Immediately the rest of my family joined me. As we prayed, Rebe and Lemma stood quietly behind us.

In a few minutes we stood up, renewed and with a fresh thought. We relived every detail of leaving the main road, coming into the acacia stand. The sun had been over *there* when we left the trail, and now it was four hours later, so our tree had to be *that* way! We followed our own directions and, sure enough, near one of the huge acacias we found the gear and the gasoline!

As Rebe and Lemma rolled the drum to the Land Rover, Rebe glanced at me. "So Allah cares about our journey after all."

I smiled. "Yes," I said. "The Lord is watching over us."

Thursday. Noon of our fourth day.

Shortly after picking up our gear, we pulled over to wait until twilight, so that as we drove through the sand dunes around the doubled-up police force at Mega we would have the protection of darkness.

The lack of food and water, and the travel over the rough riverbed, had left us exhausted. While Deme spread the

107

blanket on the ground for Mickey, I began to clean the clutter from the back of the Land Rover so Lali and Bete' would have a more comfortable place to rest. The others helped me pull the luggage out and fold stray articles of clothing. Suddenly Mickey stuck his head out.

"Look!" he shouted. "An orange! It was in the crevice on the side!"

It was small and dried-up—one we normally would have thrown away. But I gratefully accepted it from Mickey's hand. I peeled it and divided it into five parts, one for each of the boys, Rebe, and Lemma. Deme and I took none, still keeping our vow not to eat until our family was safe.

The orange was just the encouragement we needed before attempting to bypass the dangerous outpost at Mega.

The boys were soon settled for an afternoon of sleep, and the rest of us chose our spots to wait. Lemma climbed onto the canvas roof of the Land Rover. Rebe lay down under a tree near the vehicle, while Deme and I chose another tree. I had just adjusted my little gold-colored cushion behind my back when I thought of Deme's silence about the welding Rebe's friend had done. "Deme, what's wrong with that weld?"

He exhaled slowly, as though dreading to tell me. "It's a bad job. All we can do is pray we don't have much bouncing ahead of us."

"What about the sand dunes? Will the weld hold?"

He hesitated again. Finally he said, "No. I don't think so. We'll have to go through Mega itself."

"Oh, Deme. . . ." My voice was lost.

Deme took my hand into his. "We'll do what we can and leave the outcome to Him. For now, all we can do is rest."

Thursday. Late afternoon, a few hours still to go before we were to enter Mega.

As the sun was getting low, just before five o'clock, I woke up and looked around me. Rebe was awake, too. He stretched and yawned and began pacing in front of the Land Rover. Was

108

he thinking of the guns? Would we have to use them now? We had our submachine gun plus other firearms the men had brought. I closed my eyes, wondering if I could ever pull a trigger. Would I freeze at the last minute?

Rebe crawled under the Land Rover and was lying on his back, looking up.

"What are you doing?" I whispered to him, unaccountably anxious.

"There's a leak in this hose. I'm gonna fuse it. . . ."

Before I could stop him, Rebe struck a match! A yellow flash darted through the grass.

Fire!

The boys were asleep next to that barrel of gasoline in the back compartment.

Shouting "Fire!", I was suddenly on my stomach crawling desperately forward beneath the vehicle next to Rebe, smothering flames with my little cushion while he slapped at them with his hands. Deme ran up, stomping on the flames at the side of the Land Rover.

When the fire was out I collapsed for a moment, right there under the vehicle. Deme knelt to help me out, asking what had happened. But as I crawled from beneath the Land Rover, I knew I'd settled the question of whether or not I could ever use a gun. I would do whatever I had to do to protect my children.

When the excitement had settled down a bit, the men began to look again at whether our Land Rover could make it across the sand dunes. The final decision was left to Deme and me. After praying about it, Deme still felt we had no choice: we would have to drive right through Mega. And we couldn't wait until dawn again. We were getting too weak. We had to go through at first-dark.

We drove to within sight of Mega. As twilight fell Rebe pulled off the road out of sight behind a sheltering boulder. He ran his fingers through his fine hair and began to describe the situation to Deme and me. The problem, he said, was that the police had built a fence down both sides of the main road in town, forcing all traffic to be funneled past police headquarters, which would be on our right as we came into town. Our only hope lay in darkness.

"And perhaps in disguise," said Rebe. "Road crews drive Land Rovers. If we put the three men in the cab, maybe we'll look like a crew coming in."

We nodded.

"In any event," said Rebe, "is it agreed if we're waved down we will not stop?"

Deme and I nodded. The moment had come to get the guns.

My heart pounded as, in the last light, Deme attached the ammunition clip to the submachine gun and handed it to me. I took the weapon firmly. Rebe loaded handguns for himself and Deme and Lemma. "Lemma? It's time," he said.

Lemma took his gun, then helped me into the back of the dark Land Rover. My sons were silent as I settled the submachine gun across my lap. Mickey reached out to pat my arm.

I could just make out, through the little window between us and the cab, that Deme was staring at the distant lights of the town. I could almost read his mind. He was planning at least one more stop to check those bad welds and to tighten what was left of the nuts. And he was wondering what size police force we would meet, up there where those innocent lights twinkled.

We waited a while longer. At last Rebe put the Land Rover into gear and we crept forward.

Thursday night. It is past time to change shifts at police headquarters in Mega.

Most of the large force recently assigned to Mega has been called out in an action against suspected freedom fighters. A skeleton crew remains, overworked, tired. Earlier in the day an update all-points bulletin has been received about the missing senator and her family.

110

She is now known to have passed a road check Sunday night, outside Addis Ababa. She was in a black Mercedes. She is probably still in the country.

The young policeman who received the bulletin is tired and ready to go home. There is an enticing bar on the other side of the street.

Slowly, anxiously, we approached Mega. I peered through the small window into the cab. Deme sat between Rebe and Lemma and I knew that all three men had their guns ready. I slipped off the safety on the submachine gun. It made a click in the dark. The boys were silent. "Lie down," I whispered.

Up ahead now was the edge of town. Rebe slowed down. Our headlights picked up the stockade fence Rebe had told us about. It would have taken scores of men to build that fence. Ten feet high, it flanked both sides of the main road so we could not see beyond the narrow chute. Where were all the police troops! Were they behind that fence?

The Land Rover slowed almost to a stop.

"Look at that!" Rebe's voice said in the darkness.

Ahead, our lights picked out a series of trenches, shallow but effective, dug across the road. How clever! Every vehicle entering town had to slow to a crawl. At several of the trenches, I could see, there were gatelike openings in the stockade fence, and I guessed that at each of these we would find police eyes examining us.

"Keep low," I whispered again to the boys. "We can just pray they'll all think we are a work crew vehicle, three men coming in late from the country."

We maneuvered the first of the ditches with a jolt. Where were all the police? Up ahead at the biggest of the barrier trenches were two gates in the fence, one on the left and one on the right. Light shone out onto the road from each of these gates but I could see no one. Not one policeman, not even a civilian. The ghost-town silence was strangely filled with tension.

We drove down the nightmarish tunnel, our crippled vehicle pitching wildly as it bumped in and out of the trenches. How would the nuts ever hold? Now we were almost at the two gates. The one on the right, surely, led into the dreaded police station. What would we find there?

"Hold on," I said to the boys. The Land Rover almost stopped, then crept in low gear over a mound of dirt and down into the ditch on the other side. My eyes strained to see through the gate on the right. There. It was the police station.

But the room was ominously empty. There was no one at the desk. I saw the backs of a couple of men disappear through a door. What was going on? I flexed my fingers again and turned toward the other gate to our left, just as Rebe and Deme did the same.

In a glance I saw that this gate led into a bar. Lights shone brightly but there were very few customers.

Then Rebe drew in his breath sharply and gave a little yelp of surprise. I crouched as low as possible, peeking out the window over Rebe's shoulder. There, standing in the shadows next to the bar, just feet away to our left, was a *policeman!*

He moved. He was in the light now, silhouetted. He had a bottle in his hand but he was definitely interested in our vehicle. I hunched over still further. The young policeman craned his neck as if peering into the cab. Three men, driving calmly through town in a Land Rover. The young man did not move.

"He thinks we are a work crew!" I said under my breath. It was a thanksgiving prayer!

We bounced over this last of the trenches right under the gaze of the one policeman! Where was everybody? "Steady does it," Deme whispered, so softly that I could barely hear him through the window.

Up ahead now the fence stopped. The road forked. To the left lay the dark countryside, and just visible to the right a dead end road leading to government buildings and garages. Rebe, of course, would turn to the left to get us out of there.

But he didn't!

In his excitement Rebe turned the wheel of our Land Rover to the right, heading straight into the dead end of nowhere.

"I made a wrong turn!" Rebe whispered.

"It's all right, Rebe!" said Deme. His voice was calm. "Just turn around and get out. We're a work crew, remember?"

Out the rear of the Land Rover I could still see the policeman standing in the light watching us. Maybe Rebe's error in turning toward the garages helped us, confirming that we were a work crew!

"You're doing fine, Rebe," Deme said. "Just don't act nervous. Come on, come on."

Rebe swung the Land Rover around and headed down the highway in the direction of freedom. I could see Deme leaning awkwardly forward. I knew his own foot was on the accelerator.

Once we were well beyond Mega, we stopped to breathe our prayers of relief. Again the men examined the useless welds and chewed-up nuts. When I walked through the dark to take my place again in the cab, I gave the submachine gun to Lemma with a sigh. Rebe's firm voice told me that he had regained his composure. He was explaining to Deme that the mysterious missing police force could easily be out here in the country.

"We just can't stay on the main road," he said. "Too dangerous. We'll have to see what the riverbed is like here."

So one more time we took out cross-country. When we reached the riverbed again we were glad to find that a work crew had broken up the boulders for the first five or six kilometers. But then the relatively smooth bed gave out. Once again as we approached unbroken river boulders, Rebe had to speed up to get momentum. I grabbed Deme's hand as the gears protested. "Please, Lord, don't let us have to stop."

Rebe shook his head. "These are even bigger than I remembered. That wheel can't take 25 kilometers of this."

We didn't answer; we just kept praying as we bounced forward and sideways and then forward again.

In our headlights I could see the black boulders that had been worn smooth by the heavy seasonal rains. The bouncing seemed endless. Every time we lunged forward, Rebe would call out again, "There! I bet we lost the wheel on that one." But each time we managed to keep moving forward.

Finally we reached a spot where Rebe felt we could climb the bank and get back on the main track as it continued past the cliffs. Both Deme and I whispered, "Thank You, Lord," as the Land Rover reached flat ground.

As we stopped to check the nuts the vehicle seemed to shudder, as though glad to be out of the riverbed, too. Deme grabbed the flashlight and hurried around to the front wheel to check the nuts. I was right behind him. As he touched the first nut it fell off into his hand! The other one was chewed up even more than the first. There was nothing that could be done but put them back on and continue driving over the rough country trails, hoping.

At just past midnight I noticed Rebe leaning forward in the cab.

"Is anything wrong?" I asked.

He chuckled. "Wrong? Not this time. Can't you guess where we are?"

"At the border? We're there!"

I shouted to the boys in back to look outside. We were in Kenya! But Rebe's voice shut off my enthusiasm. "Don't get too excited yet," he said. "We've still got the desert."

Deme gripped my hand. "Praise the Lord anyhow, honey."

I grinned back at him in the moonlight. Rebe was right. Our real sanctuary was still far away on the other side of the desert. I remembered Rebe's saying that people had been captured *across* the border and brought back to Addis. Our ordeal wasn't over.

After we had traveled another 45 minutes, Rebe stopped so

Deme could try to tighten the wheel nuts again. Before Deme climbed out he suggested that we all give thanks to the Lord for having brought us this far. I nodded and we went to the back compartment and opened the door.

I held out my arms to our sons. "Come on. Let's give thanks."

Bete' and Mickey climbed out, but Lali stopped at the doorway. In the shadowy glow of the headlights' reflection on the ground I could see the worry in his eyes.

"Aren't we going back to Ethiopia?" he asked.

I shook my head. "Not for a long time."

A huge strangling sob came from my youngest son. He threw himself against me. That was just too much for the rest of us after all we had been through, and we began to feel our throats tighten, too. I rubbed Lali's back and begged him to stop, but he had been holding back tears for several days. They just kept coming. Finally he managed to gasp, "Why didn't you tell me we'd never come back?"

I hugged him all the harder. "But we couldn't tell you. What would you have done?"

The tears ran down his cheeks. "I would have said goodbye to my grandfather! Now I'll never see him again!"

At that his great gasping sobs started again. Deme and I cried, too. Lali was probably right. *Never* was the right word. Never again would we see Father, never again would we touch the soil of our beloved country.

Lali cried until he was exhausted. Only then could we offer thanks. Deme asked Rebe and Lemma to join us as we stood in a circle and held hands in the darkness. We expressed gratitude for having made it to this desert gateway.

Friday, 3:00 a.m. Less than an hour after crossing the border.

We were continuing to drive on the track that was our route south when suddenly the back of the Land Rover dropped to the ground with a bone-jarring jolt.

Rebe quickly turned off the motor and ran to the back.

115

Deme and I scrambled out to make sure the boys were all right. Bete' had bumped his head, but there were no serious injuries. We clustered around to look at our newest problem.

Deme shone the flashlight on the back corner of the Land Rover. The rear left wheel lay forlornly in the dirt, completely broken away from the vehicle.

Deme handed me the flashlight and got down on his knees to look more closely

"What is it?" I asked.

"Powder. They're nothing but powder."

Of course I didn't know what he was talking about. "What are nothing but powder?"

"The bearings. Look. They're pulverized."

I looked very closely, but I still didn't understand what he meant. All I knew was that we had a front wheel held on by two partially stripped bolts and a rear wheel that was off because of powdered bearings, whatever they were.

"What can we do?"

Deme's voice was tired. "For now, nothing. We'll try to sleep, and when tomorrow comes, we'll see."

Exhausted, all of us slept, unaware that our latest drama was just beginning.

Chapter Eleven

Friday. Dawn of the fifth day of our attempted escape.
With the sunrise I had to force myself to think what day it was. All our days were blending into a continuous nightmare. Had we really been on the road since Sunday night?

But I raised my hands. "Lord, thank You for watching over us during the night. Thank You that this breakdown occurred here instead of in one of the towns. Thank You for providing this day for us."

The sun woke the others. If only I had some water. We had all been weakened by this seemingly never-ending trip, but the lack of water was now a real threat. I wondered how much more we'd have to endure before we were through.

I stood next to Deme as he stared at the wheel. It looked even worse in the daylight.

"Deme, how did this happen?"

Deme answered me in the mechanic's language that I could not understand.

"Can you fix it?" I asked.

"No," Deme said, "not really. But I might find some way to hold it together until we can get to Marsabit. First of all, we need something to fill up the space taken by the bearings."

"Like what?"

"I don't know yet. We'll just have to devise something." Deme began taking inventory. "Let's think what we've got," he said. "Not much, really—a couple of glasses, a little clothing, some aluminum foil, four tin cans."

"Sounds like the parable of the loaves and fishes," I said. "Not much, and yet it has to go a long, long way."

While I talked, Deme was rummaging through the food chest. He pulled out the aluminum foil. "Marta," he said, his

117

eyes aglow, "this just might work." He began to fold the foil into tight strips. I looked at the wheel again. How was it going to be put back with only a small wrench and some folded tin foil?

When Deme had finished, he stood up. "Marta, what cosmetics did you bring? Do you have lipstick or cold cream? Anything we can use for axle grease?"

I started to shake my head. Then I remembered the Vaseline! Would that work?

Deme was delighted. He smeared Vaseline over the foil. Then all six of us—even Lali—strained to lift the left rear corner of the vehicle while Deme placed the wheel back on. Then he put the almost-stripped nut onto the almost-stripped shaft. By midmorning we were able to climb back into the Land Rover.

Deme slumped against the inside of the door. His hands, still covered with welts from insect bites, were now caked with blood. His shirt clung to him. Rebe turned the ignition key. As the vehicle slowly, slowly began to move forward, I saw that Deme was mouthing his thanks to the Lord. I took Deme's battered hand in mine, adding my prayer of thanksgiving for *him*.

Friday. Noon of the fifth day of our escape. We'd had no water since Thursday morning and we'd be in the desert in a few hours! That desert loomed an ever-larger threat as our crippled vehicle limped along.

We stopped every few kilometers. Deme tightened the bolts on the front wheel and checked the makeshift bearings on the back wheel. Each time we had to stop I noticed that Rebe's hands gripped the steering wheel with more intensity.

Finally after one stop Rebe hit the steering wheel with the heel of his hand. "I wish Wolde were here! I'd punch him in the nose! This stupid Land Rover with its stupid repairs, this stupid trip with that stupid desert waiting. . . . "

His outburst startled us. Finally Rebe was quiet, but I could see the fury in his face. We crept through the ever-drier land toward the dreaded desert. Stop. Crawl. Repair. Wait. . . .

Friday, 6:30 p.m. We had been on the road since Sunday night.
Just as the sun was setting, the rear wheel fell off again. This time Deme and Rebe were too exhausted to do anything until morning.

The boys climbed down to walk around a bit before stretching out. I worried about further damage to Mickey's liver. There was nothing to do except pray.

Deme and I sat with our backs against the Land Rover. "Deme, what will you do this time? We can't break down in the desert tomorrow."

His answer came quickly. "Well, we've used the last of the foil and the last of the electrical tape. What exactly do we have left? We have one wrench and a few small tin cans, half a jar of Vaseline, some clothing and seven very tired people. From that we will have to do what we can."

We stared into the darkness. Tomorrow, the killing desert. . . .

Saturday. Dawn. The beginning of the seventh day of our ordeal.
Finally morning arrived. For the new repairs, Deme took the empty juice cans and stomped them flat and shaped them into a metal tube around the shaft of the wheel. Again the men worked for hours. We watched the sun climb higher in the sky. We should have crossed the desert last night and would have if it hadn't been for this breakdown. But now we had no choice but to risk a day crossing. We had been out of water for more than two days and were too weak to last much longer.

I alternated between watching Deme and watching the sun. The desert waited out there, just ahead.

Saturday, 10:00 a.m.
Finally the wheel was on the vehicle again. We climbed in, straining to pull ourselves up by the door handles. Our strength was almost gone.

119

Rebe drove, continuing to grip the steering wheel in quiet fury. We had to travel slowly, slowly.

Gradually the bushes around us began to appear farther and farther apart as the sun climbed.

Saturday, 11:15 a.m.

We mounted a rise. There ahead of us, stretching out forever, was the desert.

As far away as I could see, everything was the same charcoal gray. Whether I looked to the left or to the right—everything was gray. Even the blue of the sky had suddenly turned that sickly shade; there was no life or color to it.

11:30 a.m. We started into the gray sand, hoping that the repair would hold.

11:40 a.m. Surely on the other side of the sand would be a little village where we could get water.

11:45 a.m. The Land Rover was like an oven. How dry my mouth was, and how relentlessly the sun beat down on our crippled vehicle.

And that awful grayness. As I closed my eyes against it, I could still see endless miles of deadness, feel endless heat from a gray sky pulsating on gray sand.

With each moment I could feel the energy being pulled out of me. The only way I could fight it was by thinking of that little house somewhere beyond the desert where we would find water.

12:20 p.m. And then the Land Rover broke down. All of us stumbled out to look, knowing we would see the same problem as before.

Rebe stared at the wheel, pulled crookedly away from the axle. He just gave up. "We are dead. There is no hope for us anymore. They will find our bodies swollen by the sun." He stumbled to the front of the Land Rover.

Deme turned slowly to Lemma. "We have no choice but to repair this *now.*"

Lemma jerked his head in an awkward nod and then waded

through the gray sand to get the wrench from under the front seat.

I took the now-empty Vaseline jar and rubbed my finger around the inside rim in an effort to get a bit of help for the boys' lips. All of them were listless from being cooped up in the hot back compartment. My every breath was a prayer that the repairs would soon be completed.

12:40 p.m. My sons and I couldn't stay in the baking vehicle. But we couldn't stand on the hot sand, either. We were in the Land Rover for a few minutes, then back out onto the sand, then back into the vehicle again. With each moment the four of us seemed to become weaker and weaker.

12:45 p.m. The only shade was the tiny strip made by the shadow of the Land Rover. Bete' went to lie down there.

1:00 p.m. The sun seemed to move quickly and the little patch of shade was gone. Bete' was in the sun, on that hot gray sand. Deme saw him just as I did.

"Bete', get up. You're right in the sun! Get up."

His lips swollen and cracked, his answer was a whisper. "Let me stay here, Dad. I'm all right."

He was so weak he couldn't stand up. He no longer cared. "Deme, what can we do? We must have water for him!"

1:02 p.m. As though wanting to see an oasis appear, we looked around. There was only the gray, hot sand.

"Deme, what can we do?" I was close to hysteria.

He had both hands over his face, and then suddenly he looked up. "There is water here. In the radiator! Get one of those glasses."

"Radiator water? Won't it be poison?"

He shook his head. "The Italian put in water. Just water. I saw him."

We had to take the risk. Bete' wasn't going to survive otherwise.

Deme got underneath the Land Rover to open the drain valve while I hurried to get a glass from the food chest. Another glass was broken, but I merely glanced at it.

121

1:05 p.m. Deme opened the radiator. A minute later he handed the glass back to me. It was filled with water the color of orange soda.

Deme saw me looking at the liquid. "Marta, it's just rust. But don't let him drink it—just give him enough to rinse out his mouth. That will help him."

I still wasn't sure. Maybe if I could strain it from glass to glass through a tissue. . . . I tried to hurry as I took the other glass from the chest and then placed several layers of tissue over the top. I strained the water, but what came out was just as orange.

1:10 p.m. I handed the glass to Bete'. "You mustn't drink it. Take only enough to rinse out your mouth."

He mumbled, "Yes," and meant to obey, I'm sure. But as soon as he had the water to his mouth, he drank it all!

I couldn't say anything to him; the damage was already done. Mickey was leaning against the Land Rover, his listless eyes on the glass still in Bete's hand. How he wanted some of that rusty water!

1:12 p.m. This time I would insist that only a sip of the water be taken. I asked Deme to get some more from the radiator, and again I tried to strain it through tissues. Again it came out just as orange.

When I handed the half-filled glass to Mickey, my voice was firm. "Don't drink it. Just take a little and wet your lips with it."

Why did I think he would be able to control that fierce longing for water any more than Bete' had? He drank it all before I could grab his arm.

Surely he wouldn't survive this rusty water. I looked from Mickey to Bete' and then back to Mickey again. What had I done to my sons?

I took the glass from Mickey's hand and put it back into the food chest, refusing to look at Lali. Normally Lali would have been begging for water, too, but I thanked the Lord that he didn't.

1:20 p.m. I watched my sons shuffle from sand to Land Rover cab and back to the sand again in their attempts to find a more tolerable place to wait. All of us were too weak to offer much help to the men working on the wheel.

1:30 p.m. I tried to stand behind Deme so that my shadow would protect him from the direct rays of the sun. But it did little good. I watched as he rewrapped the flattened cans and foil tighter and secured them with Mickey's belt. When he stood up, he looked around as though searching for something else.

"We need a hammer now. I've got to flatten the bearing shaft to keep all this in place."

I understood only that we needed a hammer. There was nothing around us but the gray sand. Then Deme decided to remove the back drive shaft and use that as a hammer. My admiration for his inventiveness grew by the minute.

The men took turns hammering. They were all too tired to swing with force. The clanging echoed through that lonely, gray land.

2:00 p.m. Never had my mouth been so dry. My tongue was sticking to the side of my cheek and I longed for just a little of the radiator water to moisten my cracked lips. But I didn't want to take Deme away from the repairs again. Rebe had told us back in Addis that the temperatures climbed to 120 degrees Farenheit, but I couldn't have imagined such unbearable heat.

2:10 p.m. I stumbled back to watch Lemma and Deme take turns pounding. Each blow was an extreme effort.

As I listened to the sound of the drive shaft being used as a hammer again, I felt a surprising peacefulness. "Lord, thank You that Deme has refused to give up. You know what this day will bring, and I accept whatever You have for us. All of us are in Your hands."

2:40 p.m. The noise of the hammering was silent. Then Deme's voice came in tired little grunts. "Well, that's it. When this one breaks, the whole thing is gone. There's nothing left after this."

I looked at Lemma, but he remained slumped against the vehicle. I helped the boys into the back compartment. We hoped that if there were another breakdown it would come in a place within a day's walk to safety. Then we might have a chance. But I knew that was just a fantasy.

Lemma and Rebe were exhausted beyond any usefulness, so Deme drove. We moved very slowly, waiting for the latest—and the last—breakdown.

3:00 p.m. We continued through the desert. With each turn of the wheels we listened for that thud that would mean we were stopped forever. But meter by meter we churned along the trail through the gray sand.

3:30 p.m. Gradually we began to see little scrub bushes with brown leaves. What an encouragement to see something other than that awful grayness!

3:50 p.m. We stayed on the little trail that led through the desert, still moving at our very slow pace, still stopping every few kilometers in order to look at the repairs and tighten the nuts.

Each time Deme stopped, I checked on our sons. Always I put my hand on the older boys' foreheads, remembering the rusty water.

4:15 p.m. Beyond the brown shrubs, we began to see little hills in the distance. I was especially excited because I began to think that just over that first hill would be the house where we could get a cup of water.

Closer and closer our Land Rover crawled toward that first hill. Slowly we began to climb, nearing the crest.

But when we got to the top, we saw only another hill. Well, the house would surely be just over that next hill. But hill after hill passed, and the little house didn't appear.

On and on we went, still waiting for our vehicle to plop down and refuse ever to move again.

I know now that it wasn't the repairs that caused the Land Rover to keep churning on; the Lord was holding that wheel on.

Saturday, 5:30 p.m.

We passed a section of highway under construction, but the workers had left for the day. The Land Rover limped on.

And then we climbed one more hill.

Suddenly in the distance we could see definite shapes—perhaps houses.

We wanted to hurry toward them, but our Land Rover continued its wounded limping.

Gradually the shapes emerged as roofs and walls. Windows. Doors. As we got closer, we could tell it was some kind of laborers' camp.

As we crept closer, we could see that the workers had their families with them, living in the small quarters.

Several people saw us and watched our vehicle limp toward them.

By the time we arrived at the cluster of homes there were a dozen handsome Kenyans waiting for us.

A dark young woman in a beige linen dress stood in front of the others. On her hip was a beautiful, fat little baby.

I leaned over and kissed Deme's unshaven cheek. The presence of that new life on his mother's hip said more to me than the woman could have known.

We had found sanctuary.

Since Then

Today in our home in Fort Wayne, Indiana, are three objects that survived our escape. The picture of His Majesty sits in a place of honor near the sofa in our living room. The one pink crystal glass is on the shelf of our china cabinet. The blue and white tablecloth lies folded in our linen drawer. All remind us of our ordeal and of the Lord's protection.

The sense of wonder at our family's escape didn't end with the sight of that beautiful Kenyan baby. For one thing, we learned that on Friday night of our journey, when the Land Rover broke down, we had been in a game preserve: all around us, unseen and dangerous lions would have been prowling. For another, when we arrived in Nairobi and had doctors examine the boys, they found no sign of damage from drinking the radiator water. Astonishingly, they also found no signs of hepatitis in Mickey. He was healthy.

While in Nairobi, we also learned from a friend just how close to arrest we had been. We truly had been sheltered by the King throughout our ordeal.

But now my family and I were refugees. We stayed in a small Nairobi hotel for two-and-a-half months awaiting permission to enter Greece, and an additional seven poverty-filled months in Athens. We were waiting to hear that we had been accepted by the United States government and that a church was willing to sponsor us.

Meanwhile, events moved ahead in Ethiopia. Our country has fallen further and further under the influence of the Soviet bloc. Gera is safe for the present; and even though she's heartsick at events in our homeland, she is unwilling to leave.

Rebe and Lemma returned to Addis. Assafa went back to his family in the country. Father is still alive, praying for our people in his little house, cared for by relatives. Our home in Addis Ababa is now being used by the government.

And the idealistic students who were so hopeful? When they no longer served the Committee, they were killed. On many occasions students were shot in front of their parents, who then were required to pay for the bullets. At another time dozens were bound together and blown up with dynamite.

Finally a church in the United States agreed to sponsor us. Eleven months after our escape, Deme, Lali, Bete', Mickey and I arrived in Fort Wayne, Indiana, where we were reunited with Sammy. But the best of all family news came when I was also reunited with a very special girl named Priscilla, born 25 years earlier. But that's a subject for another book. Our family continues to enjoy that special closeness which often comes out of intense trial.

Deme and I know at least a little now about why we were allowed to escape.

First of all, we got out in order to tell the story behind the headlines about the takeover of Ethiopia. But what is more significant, we are involved in telling of the plight of other refugees. Our escape took place just at the beginning of a major exodus. Thousands fled. Where would they go?

The Sudan, with the help of the United Nations, was the first nation to establish camps for those who walked across the border. The refugees came with nothing and with no place to go. They wait for their one food ration each day—sitting in the hot sun or seasonal rains. They wait, wait, endlessly wait, looking for something to provide hope, most not even daring to dream of a sponsor.

Deme and I decided to do what we could to help. We drew on the limited resources of a small business we established in Fort Wayne, but this was not nearly enough. With the help of dedicated Christians, we have established a program called

127

Project Mercy. Occasionally we send food and clothing to the camps. But our main effort is to tell of the refugees' plight to any who will help. Above all, we tirelessly seek refugee sponsors.

It seems an impossible task. But our survival in the desert was an impossibility, too. We continue to do what we can—and we still leave the outcome to the Lord.

If you would like more information about our work, please write:

PROJECT MERCY
~~P.O. Box 5515~~
~~Fort Wayne, Indiana 46825~~

PROJECT MERCY
7011 Ardmore Ave.
Fort Wayne, IN 46809

128